HEAVEN KNOWS I'M MISERABLE NOW

By Colin Smith

First published (Paperback) in the UK in 2016
by Violet Circle Publishing.

Manchester, England, UK.

ISBN: 978-1-910299-16-6

British Library Cataloguing in Publication Data.
A catalogue record for this book is available from the British Library.

All papers used in the production of this book are sourced only from wood grown in sustainable forests.

www.violetcirclepublishing.co.uk

Dedicated to:

Mum and Dad
Carl Morgan
Nigel Marland
Keith and Judith Smith

The Author Colin Smith.

Born in Manchester, settled in Dukinfield, Cheshire, and has lived and worked locally all his life.

Colin has always been interested and involved in creative pursuits; acting, music, photography and writing. He appeared in his first theatrical production aged fourteen, and has to date, appeared in close to one hundred productions, of one kind or another. He is still involved in paid and unpaid acting work, and currently plays 'Alf Bradshaw' in 'The Bradshaw's' touring stage show.

Colin has played in a number of bands in the Manchester area including playing live on stage and in the recording studio over many years. He has also been involved in radio broadcasting, and currently is employed as a professional photographer.

Colin's interest in writing started in 2009, where he wrote two plays just before attending Salford University, where he focused on writing Performance (Hons) degree. He graduated with a 'First' in 2012.

In 2010 his second play 'Heaven Knows I'm Miserable Now' was performed for the first time in Oldham's Lyceum Theatre. It was a big hit, and won an award at the 'Greater Manchester Drama Federation'. Since then three more productions of 'Heaven Knows' have been performed in Manchester and Liverpool, and Colin has written several other scripts which have been performed locally as well as in Australia, The Caribbean, and South America. 'Heaven Knows' is his first published play, and hopefully the first of many to come.

A Brief History of The Play

2008 was a difficult time. The death of my father, redundancy and a marriage break up left me at a very low ebb, and I had difficulty motivating myself. The future looked bleak and I needed a distraction.

For some strange reason, I started to develop an idea about a man who dies and goes to the afterlife. I thought about the notion of meeting our loved ones on the other side, and wondered what would happen to someone who'd been widowed? I then considered the idea that someone, (if a little unlucky) could in theory, have been widowed twice, or even thrice. I know some people believe they will be reunited with partners when they die, but if they had two or three ex-wives... what then? It seemed like the basis for a funny script.

I hadn't written a play before, but I have been involved with the theatre all my life, (mostly acting) and knew how a play was structured and paced, and also how to develop characters. I started putting ideas on a page, and carried an 'ideas book' around with me to get some kind of structure to my story. I had decided my central character would be a kind of everyman. I figured he would need to be in his 60s or 70s if he were to have been widowed three times. I named him Andy.

Sitting alone in my kitchen, I began writing. I found myself laughing at my own jokes, and felt the whole thing was rather inspired, as ideas and jokes were coming thick and fast. I decided that Andy is to be 'collected' from life by a dim-witted 'collector' and then subjected to a couple of amusing interviews in the afterlife. He is then taken to a temporary residence before meeting his three wives, where he discovers he will be staying with Adolph Hitler and Jesus Christ. Whilst there he meets up with wives one, two and three in sequence, and this would be a great opportunity for comedy; with Hitler, Christ, and the wives, who are not what Andy expects, as they are all 'projecting' the image they see of themselves in the afterlife.

I finished the first draft in late 2008, and on Christmas Day we read it around my brother's kitchen table, with family and friends reading the parts. Everyone was laughing, and thought I was on to something funny and original. In the New Year, I took it to a local theatre (Lyceum Theatre Oldham) and asked if they would allow their actors to come down and read it; just to hear how it sounded with more experienced actors. That night, after the reading, the artistic director asked me if they could put the play on there as part of their next season. It was more than I could have hoped for.

In September 2010 the play hit the stage, tickets sold like hot cakes, and the show was completely sold out. Audiences loved it and we went on to win an award at The Manchester Drama Federation for 'Adventure in Theatre'.

Since then 'Guide Bridge Theatre' produced it in 2012, 'Saddleworth Players' in 2013, and more recently, for the first time a theatre outside the Manchester area, 'The Waterloo and Crosby Theatre Company' produced it in 2016.

For all inquiries for production of this play please contact:
colinsmith_photography@yahoo.co.uk

'Heaven Knows I'm Miserable Now' was first performed by Oldham's 'Lyceum Players' in September 2010 with the following cast.

Andy...Kevin Grocock
Eva...Natalie Smith
Errol...Roger Hartmann
Ann...Judith Redkwa
Todd...Edmund Taylor
Kurt...Peter Fitton
Jesus...Colin Smith
Hitler...Damien Kavanagh
Emma...Amy Turner
Mandy...Amy Turner
Vicky...Jason Sharp
Roger...Roger Hartmann
Kerry...Helen Schutzmann
Young Andy...Edmund Taylor

Directed by NIGEL MARLAND

Stage Manager:	Judith Redkwa
Lighting:	Sue Wharf, Ian Taylor
Sound:	Scott Kempton, Gavin Mitchell
Wardrobe:	Terri Parker
Original artwork:	Chris Cunday

ACT ONE
Scene One

Time: Winter. The 2012.

Music: 'If Paradise is Half as Nice' by 'The Amen Corner'.

A bedroom. Andy, a very ordinary looking man in his late sixties is asleep in bed. He is snoring loudly. Next to him is a stunning looking blonde…Eva. She is perhaps in her early twenties. She is sitting up reading a book. There is very little light in the room, just some street light from the window. Andy snorts and rolls over. Eva looks at her watch then looks in a small notebook she has on the bedside table. Andy is wearing pyjamas. She is wearing sexy night attire. Eva looks at her watch again and makes a note in her notebook. Andy stops snoring. Eva puts the book down. Andy starts to stir. He opens his eyes slowly and lets out a slow moan. Eva remains still. Suddenly Andy sees Eva and bolts upright.

Andy: My God!

Eva: *(Sweetly)* Hi.

Andy: Who the devil are you?

Andy leaps out of his bed.

Eva: I'm Eva.

Andy turns on the light and sees this gorgeous figure in his bed.

Andy: What are you doing in my bed?

Eva: Oh, don't you like that approach?

Andy: How did you get in my house?

Eva: Through the window.

Andy: That's not possible. I always lock it. So, come on, how did you get in?

Eva: You do ask a lot of questions, don't you?

Andy: I just want to know who you are and how you got here. As you are in my house and in my bed, that doesn't seem an unreasonable question.

Eva: Isn't that two questions?

She gets out of bed and walks up to Andy.

Eva: When was the last time you woke up to find a strange...and if I may say so... attractive, vivacious young fox like me in your bed? I bet it doesn't happen every day, does it?

Andy: You know, I'm struggling to think of the last time it *did* happen; might have been a week last Tuesday.

Eva: Really?

Andy: No...That was a joke.

Eva: You see, a lot of men wouldn't think to ask how I got here. Some men don't care about such details.

Andy: You mean you do this a lot?

Eva: All the time.

Andy: Are you a prostitute?

Eva: *(Slapping him, then calmly)* No.

Andy: You do this all the time?

Eva: Yes.

Andy: Why?

Eva: It's what I do.

Andy: What you do?

Eva : Yes.

Andy: Why?

Eva: Someone has to do it.

Andy: Do they?

Eva: Of course they do, silly.

Eva struts around, to give Andy a full view of her sexy nightwear.

Eva: So, what do you think of this little number?

Looking at Eva, a shade embarrassed.

Andy: It's...very...err...nice.

Eva: Nice! Is that all you've got to say? It's meant to

be jaw-droppingly sexy. It's meant to make you salivate like an elephant with a fire hydrant up its bottom.

Andy: *(Puzzled)* ...?

Eva: So, what did you think of the whole, 'getting into bed thing', did you like that approach?

Andy: I don't know, I'm at a loss. You say, it's what you do...to get into bed with men in the middle of the night without any explanation of how you got here.

Eva: Oh no, you misunderstood me. I don't normally get into bed with men in the middle of the night, that's just an approach I thought I'd try. You see, I've been working on ways of improving my method of meeting my clients. I've tried all sorts of ways. Walking up to them on the street, or appearing in the bath or shower with them. Whatever I do, it always takes them by surprise.

Andy: I'll bet!

Eva: So, I thought...I know! I'll slip into bed with my next client wearing a nice sexy negligee and see how that goes. So, here I am!

Andy: You keep saying 'client'...are you sure you're not a prostitute?

Eva: *(Slapping him...then calmly)* No.

Andy: Did one of my mates at the British Legion put you up to this? It wasn't Edgar, was it?

Eva: Edgar?

Andy: He's a bit of a prankster. I wouldn't put it past him to be behind this.

Eva: Is he one of *us*?

Andy: Us? I suppose that depends on who '*us'* is, as it were. Who *is* 'us'?

Eva: You what?

Andy: Will you please just tell me who you are?

Eva: Eva.

Andy: I know *that*!

Eva: Sorry, I can't remember if I mentioned it or not. I'm such a scatterbrain. It's a good job I've got my little book.

Andy: Your little book?

Eva: My 'little book of what's what'. If I need to know something about something, I put it in there. For example, did you know that Guy Fawkes has an irrational fear of Woody Woodpecker?

Andy shakes his head.

Andy: Has anyone ever told you you're a very strange girl?

Eva: Yes! But you must admit I'm 'hot', aren't I? Do you find me appealing? Do I 'float your boat'?

Andy: You're a very attractive girl, certainly. Is it your intension to try and...you know?

Eva: What?

Andy: Well…to…do I have to spell it out?

Eva: Yes, please.

Andy: You don't make things easy, do you?

Eva: Well, it's not my intention to make things hard.

Andy: *(Looking at Eva in her sexy nightwear)* You could have fooled me!

Eva: You see, I thought as a man who's been married three times, you'd be more receptive to a scantily clad 'bimbo'.

Andy: How do you know about that?

Eva: What?

Andy: That I've been married three times.

Eva: It's on your records, silly.

Andy: My records? What records?

Eva: You know, I think what I'll do next time is tap on the window. That might not be such a big shock.

Andy: I wouldn't tap on the window at *(He looks at his watch)* four-fifteen in the morning if I were you.

Eva: It's not four-fifteen.

Andy: *(Looking at his watch again)* Yes it is!

Eva: Your watch has stopped; they always do.

Andy: Look, Eva. Can we please cut to the chase?

Eva: I'm not going to chase you! It's not a farce! *(She looks around)* Now, where is my little book of 'what's what'?

She picks up the book from the bedside table and flicks through it.

Eva: Let me see…You are Carlos Saspereller…Oh no, that's not right. Hang on. You are Andrew Reardon, aged sixty-seven of seventeen Wordsworth Avenue, are you not?

Andy: Yes.

Eva: Thank goodness for that! I got it right… hurray! That's one in the 'win column'.

Andy looks puzzled.

Eva: Anyway, time we weren't here.

Andy: Time *you* weren't here, certainly. I'll see you to the door. It's been a pleasure to meet you, Eva. Parting is such sweet sorrow. I'll show you out. Err… do you have anything else to wear? You can't go out dressed like that! Where are your other clothes?

Eva: I don't have any.

Andy: What did you wear when you came here?

Eva: This *is* what I was wearing. I came 'suited and booted', as they say.

Andy: Didn't you even have a coat?

Eva: A coat? That's not very seductive.

Andy: It's November, for one thing and then there's the little matter of your modesty.

Eva: Who's she?

Andy: Look, you can't go out on the street dressed like that. Someone will assault you. Besides, it's a cold night; you'll catch your death.

Eva slaps her forehead.

Eva: Oh, you've just reminded me.
Andy: What?

Eva: I told you I was a bit forgetful…You… you have to come with me.

Andy: I think not!

Eva: Yes, I should have mentioned at the start. You and I are going off together.

Andy: Well, that's a very tempting offer. However... tempting as that offer might be on the face of it. It is my considered opinion that you are 'bonkers'! I mean that in the nicest possible way, of course.

Eva: Thank you…I think.

Andy: I have a coat you can borrow. Now, let me escort you to the door.

Eva: You don't understand. *You* have to come with

me; it's the 'way of things'.

Andy: Look...Eva. I'm not going anywhere with you and that's that!

Eva: Oh, my giddy aunt! I'm beginning to think The Grim Reaper had the right idea. No one ever argued with him. He'd turn up with his scythe and his 'no nonsense' approach. He'd point that bony finger and no one said 'diddley'. I try to do it nicely...get myself all scrubbed up...wear this very revealing outfit and look what happens? I get accused of being a hornet.

Andy: Harlot.

Eva: Whatever.

Andy: *(Sarcastically)* The Grim Reaper?

Eva: You've heard of him?

Andy: I've heard of The Grim Reaper, yes. Is he a friend of yours?

Eva: Not really, more of an acquaintance. I've met him a couple of times; doesn't say much but very charismatic.

Andy shakes his head.

Andy: You really are 'away with the fairies' aren't you?

Eva: You don't believe in fairies, do you?

Andy: *(Sarcastically)* Oh, no, but I've had sushi with Santa Claus a couple of times, and I once went to

'Spud-u-like' with John the Baptist.

Eva giggles.

Eva: You're silly.

Andy: Thank you.

Eva: Shall we go, then?

Andy: I'd rather stay here, if it's all the same to you.

Eva: Sorry, no can do…Take my hand.

Andy: What?

Before Andy can protest Eva takes his hand.

Eva: Now just relax and think of nice fluffy woodland animals with massive eyes.

Andy: Oh God, I feel all light-headed. What's happening to me?

Eva: Relax, it's perfectly normal. We're crossing over, that's all.

Andy: I can see a door. Where did that come from? Oh. Lord, I feel dizzy. What's going on?
Eva: Don't worry…We're not in your house anymore.
Andy: *(Flustered)* What's happening to me?

Andy lets out a yell.

Blackout.

ACT ONE
Scene Two

***Music**: 'The Voyage' by 'The Moody Blues'.*

A room. Andy is lying on the floor. He is still wearing his pyjamas. He comes to and looks around. The first thing he sees is a desk with a man, Errol sitting behind it. Errol is a slightly overweight, cheery, camp chap. Andy gets up a little bleary. Errol smiles at him.

Errol: How are you? Oh, silly question! *(He laughs)*

Andy: *(Still half asleep)* Where am I?

Errol: Oh dear. I was hoping you might surprise me and say something more original. You know, more people say "Where am I?" than anything else. It's the most popular phrase upon waking up here.

Andy: Err...

Errol: First time?

Andy: Err...

Errol: *(He laughs)* I'm kidding.

Andy: What's going on? Where is this place? Oh, my head!

Errol: Don't worry, dear, everything will be explained to you in good time. Now, don't be afraid, approach the desk, I don't bite, well...unless you want me to. *(He laughs)*

Andy approaches Errol's desk.

Errol: Now then, I'm Errol. Let's get a few details about you to be getting on with, shall we? Then we can get you all sorted out and all lovely, can't we?

Andy: Err…

Errol: Right. Let's start with an easy one…name?

Andy: Err…Andy, Andrew Reardon.

Errol: Oh, same as the snooker player, you know… Dracula?

Andy: What?

Errol: *(Looking on the computer)* Reardon? Oh yes, here we are, Andrew Reardon, yes, we've got your mug-shot. Oh, don't you look grumpy? Born the third of September, 1945. Is that correct?

Andy: Yes.

Errol: Now, have you got the precise time of death?

Andy: I beg your pardon?

Errol: Time of death?

Andy: What are you talking about?

Errol: What time did you expire?

Andy: Expire?

Errol: Yes, dear. Your watch…what time does it say?

Andy: Err *(He looks)* Four-fifteen.

Errol: Right, we're off...Lovely. *Cause* of death?

Andy: Cause of death?

Errol: Yes, dear.

Andy: Is this some sort of joke?

Errol: No, dear. Cause of death?

Andy: Are you trying to imply that I'm dead? Is that what all this nonsense is about?

Errol: Yes, my love, except I'm not implying it. It is simply a fact of life.

Andy: I'm afraid I don't think I'm actually dead, if you want the truth of it.

Errol: Denial! A perfectly natural reaction. So…cause of death?

Andy: I'm *not* dead!

Errol: Yes, you are!

Andy: No, I'm not!

Errol: Listen, petal, you wouldn't *be* here if you weren't dead. Now don't be stroppy. Just tell me how you died.

Andy: Well, when I *do* die, I'll let you know.

Errol: Oh, stubborn as a mule! Look, what did your collector say?

Andy: My collector? I don't *have* a collector.

Errol: That's how you got here. Did he/she not explain that to you?

Andy: Wait a minute, you don't mean that dizzy Eva, do you? She came to my house. I think it was last night; it's all a bit vague.

Errol: Eva? Yes, no wonder you're a bit confused. Where were you when she arrived?

Andy: Well, I was asleep.

Errol: In bed?

Andy: Yes.

Errol: Now we're getting somewhere. Were you ill?

Andy: No.

Errol: Did you have a dickey ticker?

Andy: I beg your pardon.

Errol: Did you have a heart attack?

Andy: What sort of question is that? This is ridiculous! Is there someone else I can talk to?

Errol: You weren't murdered or anything like that, were you?

Andy: Of course not. Look, for the last time, I'm *not dead*!

Errol: Did a plane hit your house or a tree or something?

Andy: *(Sharply)* NO!

Errol: All right dear, don't get your knickers in a tangle. I'll put 'died in his sleep'. We'll have to check Eva's records for confirmation...if she doesn't lose them. *(He types on the computer)* So, Andrew Reardon, aged sixty seven. Occupation...Porn star... is that correct?

Andy: What?

Errol: *(He laughs)* I'm kidding! I like to liven the job up a bit, you know. It gets a bit tedious. I see you were a painter/decorator, is that right?

Andy: Will you please stop talking about me in the past tense?

Errol: Well, I'm afraid it *is* the past tense now, flower. No need for painter/decorators here. You can't earn a living when you're not alive, can you? *(He laughs again. He looks at the screen)* Oh, I see you were married three times. Heavens to Betsy!

Andy: Yes.

Errol: All of them predeceased you?

Andy: That's right.

Errol: What a funny old business.

Andy: Yes, well, that's one way of putting it.

Errol: Have you thought about what you're going to do?

Andy: About what?

Errol: About your spouses.

Andy: I'm not with you.

Errol: Well, you've got three of them, haven't you? You've got a lot to think about.

Andy: Err…

Errol: Well, I've got enough information for now, sweetness. If you'd just like to take a seat with those lovely people over there, someone will call your name in two shakes of a donkey's tail, all right? Thank you so much for your co-operation.

Andy: Oh, that's it for now, is it?

Errol: Yes. Take a seat.

Andy looks round and sees two people sitting in chairs waiting. One is Todd, a young, gaunt looking man in his early twenties. The other, Ann, is a woman in her late fifties/early sixties, dressed in wedding attire. Ann is folding her arms and has a face like thunder. Andy takes the seat in-between them. Todd is staring into space. Ann looks Andy up and down.

Andy:*(To Todd)* Hello.

Todd ignores him.

Andy: *(To Ann)* Hello.

Ann: *(Grumpily)* Hello.

Andy: I'm Andy.

Ann: Ann.

Andy: This is a right old 'to-do', isn't it?

Ann: Excuse me?

Andy: This...It's a right old pickle.

Ann: You do realise that we are in fact...'dead', don't you?

Andy: Well, it's starting to look that way.

Ann: I'll have you know, I'm upset! In fact, I'm *very* upset! Very upset indeed! And I don't honestly think that the term 'right old to-do' quite sums up the gravity of this situation...do you?

Andy: I suppose not. I'm sorry; I don't know what else to say. I've never been dead before. What are you supposed to say?

Ann: It's a tragedy...that's what it is!

Andy Yes, well, I can see why you would say that. Death is always tragic... especially your own.

Ann: I can't be dead! It's not convenient! I want to see someone about it. I need to make some calls.

Andy: Who you gonna call?

Todd: *(Deadpan)* 'Ghostbusters'.

Ann: My God! That's the first time he's said anything.

Andy: I'll admit this is upsetting. I mean, they say we're dead. You don't look dead to me. In my book, dead is meant to be final; The big sleep! Lights out, etc, but here we are in this room…waiting for God-knows-what, with some cheeky young scamp, making flippant remarks about our misfortune.

Ann: Misfortune! My God! We have the 'master of understatement' in our midst. I'd say it was a bit more than misfortune to have your life snatched away in your prime...wouldn't you?

Andy: I would agree, except that we are not dead in the lifeless corpse sense of the word, but dead in the 'afterlife' sense of the word, and as it stands, we're yet to discover what life, or more accurately 'afterlife' has in store.

Ann: That's all well and good but what about my husband and my children? I was at my son's wedding for God's sake…choked on a flippin' chicken bone! That'll have put a dampener on the celebrations. How can you expect the best man to tailor his speech to that turn of events? On top of that, this hat cost me a fortune. Then there's my young grandson…what about him?

Andy: Well, we'll just have to see what comes out in the wash.

Ann: I don't *want* to be dead! I don't mean to be negative but I just *know* I'm not going to like it.

Andy: I'm not over keen myself but I suppose we're all just going to have to try to make the best of a bad situation.

Ann: *(To Todd)* I'm going to kill him in a minute.

Todd: Too late!

Ann : Oh, yes. Damn!

Andy: Look, I'm sorry. I'm just trying to stay 'upbeat'.

Ann: *(Livid) 'Upbeat'*? How can you be 'upbeat' about having snuffed it? You really are an irritating little man. Can't you just keep your understated comments to yourself?

Andy: Sorry. I just seem to keep upsetting you with everything I say. Perhaps it might be for the best if I keep quiet.

Ann: I think that might be a good idea.

There is a long, uncomfortable pause. Andy looks at Todd and smiles at him. Todd does not respond. Ann is trying to use her mobile phone.

Andy: *(To Todd)* Hello.

Todd does not respond.

Andy: You're a bit on the young side to be in a place like this, aren't ya?

Todd looks at Andy with a blank stare.

Andy: You don't have to tell me if you don't want.

Pause. Todd stares blankly at Andy.

Todd: Have you ever really considered...death?

Andy: I don't know what you mean...considered it?

Todd: I believed death was the end…the final escape into darkness…Not so. When we talk of death, we mean death in the sense of what one might have expected it to be…nothing! One would not anticipate death being a new form of existence… or a different form of consciousness from life as we know it…or knew it. Death equals life, or at least, if it were death then...what is it? If this death is in fact life, then what is death? How do we find death within death which appears to be life? If death is not death...as appears to be the case… then what is? If death, that is to say, *this…* that we find ourselves in… is the end of the beginning, then what is the beginning of the end? Is there an end? Is there an end of the end? And if so…what is it?

Andy: Come again.

Ann: He's barking mad!

Todd: Todd.

Andy: How do you do?

Todd: I do rather badly, I'm afraid.

Andy: I hope we're not going to start to decompose, like in those Zombie movies. I hope we're not going to go walking the streets moaning and trying to eat people. That kind of behaviour lacks dignity.

Ann: I do wish you'd shut up!

Andy: Sorry, the thought just popped into my head.

Todd lets out a painful and sudden sob.

Andy: Great Scott!

Todd: That had to come out.

Ann: I think I preferred it when you were quiet. *(To Andy)* When I arrived here, he was sat there...didn't say a 'dickey bird'. Since then, everything he has said has been complete drivel. I've not exactly had the best time of it but ending up with you two is the icing on the cake.

Todd: This is a bad, bad situation.

Ann: Tell me something I *don't* know.

Todd: My brother owns a chinchilla called Reg.

Ann: What?

Todd: That's something you don't know.

Andy: A bad, bad situation, what do you mean?

Todd: Life is bad but death is worse. We have an escape from life; at least, we thought we did. Now we realise that that escape is not escape at all. There is no escape.

Andy: How did you get here?

Todd: I committed suicide.

Andy: Blood and sand!

Todd: So, you see. It's worse for me than it is for you. I wanted eternal blackness...not this.

Ann: Are we supposed to feel sorry for you? You *wanted* to die. I had everything to live for.

Todd: So what are you complaining about? Don't complain about being dead if death as we know it now, is in fact life. If death is really life, then…

Andy: *(Interrupting)* Yes, well, let's not get into all that again, shall we.

Ann: This is an intolerable state of affairs. I need someone to blame! And that man won't tell me anything. I've tried 'til I was blue in the face.

Todd: Interesting turn of phrase for a corpse.

Ann gives him a dirty look. Todd shrugs.

Ann: To cap it all, I can't get a signal on my mobile.

Andy: Maybe we can escape.

Ann: Escape?

Andy: Yes, go back home. I came in through a door somewhere. What if we can find that door and just go back through it.

Todd: You can't.

Andy: How do you know?

Todd: Because I hung my mortal body; it's swinging from a girder in a disused warehouse in Timperley. That's how I got here. I have to accept that that plane of existence is no longer open to me. The world as we know it has gone.

Ann lets out a muted cry.

Andy: Maybe this room represents a kind of limbo between life and death. Perhaps that's where we are now. You hear about people being brought back to life after they've died. Perhaps if we can find that door quickly before it's too late. Before they send us, wherever they're going to send us, we can wake up back at home. I can meet my friend Edgar at the British Legion and we can play crib as planned.

Errol: Andrew Reardon.

Andy: Err…yes.

Errol: Time for your evaluation.

Andy: Oh, crikey!

Errol: Room five thousand eight hundred and seventy-seven….. B.

Andy: What?

Errol: *(Pointing)* It's just there.

Ann: That's not fair. I was here first.

Andy gets up and walks to the door.

Andy: Ah, well. Here goes nothing.

Blackout.

ACT ONE
Scene Three

Music: *'My Death' by 'Scott Walker'*

A room. A sharp-suited man with small round glasses is sitting behind a desk, Kurt. He is a no-nonsense, humourless man who does not smile. When he asks his questions, he generally does so quickly, giving Andy little time to think. Then he will pause to make Andy squirm. Andy enters the room nervously. Kurt is writing. He looks up at Andy. Andy smiles. Kurt does not respond in any way. Andy clears his throat.

Kurt: What do you want?

Andy: They told me to come in here.

Kurt: Who did?

Andy: That man.

Kurt: What man?

Andy: The man behind the desk.

Kurt: Who was he?

Andy: I've no idea.

Kurt: If you didn't know who he was, why did you do what he said?

Andy: Err…I'm not sure. He kept saying I was dead.

Kurt: Who did?

Andy: That man.

Kurt: What man?

Andy: The one behind the desk.

Kurt: Do you think that you're dead?

Andy: Well…I don't know…Am I?

Kurt: Why are you asking me?

Andy: You look like someone in charge.

Kurt: If you're the sort of person who doesn't know if he's alive or dead, then God help you.

Pause.

Kurt: Take a seat.

Andy: *(Sitting in the chair at the desk)* Thank you.

Kurt: Andrew Reardon.

Andy: That's right. You *do* know who I am.

Kurt: I have some questions for you.

Andy: Yes.

Kurt: You will make things a lot easier for yourself if you answer the questions quickly and honestly. Do you understand?

Andy: Yes.

Kurt: Understand *this*. You must *not* lie to me…is that clear?

Andy: Right, yes.

Kurt: Do *you* have any questions?

Andy: Err…lots…yes.

Kurt: I mean, about what I just said?

Andy: Not about that, no.

Kurt: Very well, we'll begin. Are you ready?

Andy: Yes. I'm ready. Fire away.

Kurt stares at him for a moment and writes something down in his pad.

Kurt: Saint or sinner?

Andy: What?

Kurt: Saint or sinner?

Andy: I don't really understand the question.

Kurt: Saint or sinner?

Andy: I'm not really either. I'm no saint but I wouldn't call myself a sinner. I've done bad things from time to time but haven't we all? I'm somewhere in the middle, I suppose.

Kurt writes something down in his pad.

Kurt: Directly or indirectly, how many people's deaths are you responsible for?

Andy: Deaths? Well, none. I'm not responsible for anyone's death. What sort of question is *that*?

Kurt: Directly or indirectly, how many animals deaths are you responsible for?

Andy: Animals? I've never killed an animal...well, I once ran over a hedgehog in Slapton but that was an accident.

Kurt: Indirectly?

Andy: That was the only time. By the time I'd seen it, it was too late.

Kurt: Indirectly?

Andy: I don't understand. I've answered the question.

Kurt: Do you like lamb chops, bacon, sausage, chicken nuggets?

Andy: Yes, of course.

Kurt: So, how many?

Andy: Oh, I see where you're coming from. You mean how many animals have I eaten in my life. Well, that's a tough question.

Kurt: How many?

Andy: I don't know.

Kurt: More than a hundred?

Andy: I would think so.

Kurt: More than a thousand?

Andy: I don't know. I didn't…I've never really thought about it. I like a bit of chicken, what's wrong with that? Who doesn't like a bit of chicken?

Kurt: More than a million?

Andy: I don't think so, not more than a million. Look, what are these questions leading to?

Kurt writes something down.

Kurt: Directly or indirectly, how many insects deaths are you responsible for?

Andy: Insects? Don't tell me you're going to penalise me for swotting a fly.

Kurt: Please answer the question.

Andy: This is insane! How would anyone know *that*? Insects are just…

Kurt: Insects are just *what*…Mister Reardon?

Andy: Err...well...

Kurt once again makes notes.

Kurt Would you mind telling me who 'Wasp Man Brian' was?

Andy 'Wasp Man Brian'? Oh yes, Brian, he was a chap who came to sort out that wasps nest in our loft.

Kurt Would you mind explaining what you mean by

'sort out'?

Andy Err…well…we were getting a lot of problems with wasps and it turned out we had a wasps nest in our loft, so, we asked Brian to…err…to

Kurt To what?

Andy To…well…

Pause.

Kurt: Is it not true that...under your instructions, 'Wasp Man Brian', as you call him, did knowingly assassinate an entire wasp colony with all the coldness of a professional hit-man?

Andy: I wouldn't have put it like that. That's ridiculous! Don't tell me that's going to get me in trouble up here? What would you have done? They were all over the place. They were a nuisance.

Kurt writes some more notes.

Kurt: Have you ever hurt an animal for your own amusement? Have you, for example...set fire to a camel?

Andy: Of course not.

Kurt: Have you ever laughed at trees?

Andy: No.

Kurt: Is it your belief that Humpty Dumpty was, in fact...an egg?

Andy: Err...?

Kurt: Do you believe in God?

Andy: I don't know.

Kurt: Do you believe in the Devil?

Andy: I don't think so.

Kurt: Have you ever praised the Lord?

Andy: Not really.

Kurt: Have you ever sung the praises of Lucifer?

Andy: No.

Kurt: Have you ever *cursed* the Lord?

Andy: No.

Kurt: Are you sure?

Andy: Yes.

Kurt: Have you ever purchased an effigy of Satan which you have then given as a gift during a romantic ritual, in the hope of using said image of 'The Dark One' to procure, directly or indirectly, sexual favours?

Andy: Of course not!

Kurt produces a 'Horny Devil' toy from under the desk.

Kurt: Then, would you mind explaining…this?

He places it on the desk.

Andy: It's a 'Horny Devil', I got it on Valentine's Day for.......

Kurt: Horny.....?

Andy: *(Sheepishly)*.....Devil.

Kurt writes more notes.

Kurt: How many of the Seven Deadly Sins have you committed?

Andy: I'm really not sure.

Kurt: Are you familiar with the Seven Deadly Sins?

Andy: Yes, sort of.

Kurt: So, how many?

Andy: I've no idea. I don't make mental notes of these things.

Kurt makes another note.

Kurt: How many of the Ten Commandments have you broken?

Andy: *(Exasperated)* Oh, God!

Kurt: I'm sorry, what did you say?

Andy: Err...nothing.

Kurt: I thought you said you never cursed the Lord.

Andy: I don't!

Kurt: You just did!

Andy: No, I didn't!

Kurt: You just said, "Oh God!" Now, if that isn't cursing then I'd like to know what is.

Andy: I didn't mean it in that way.

Kurt: Well, how *did* you mean it, Mister Reardon?

Andy: It's not like I said that "God was a bit daft" or "God was a puff" or something offensive like that.

Kurt: Are you homophobic, Mister Reardon?

Andy: No, of course I'm not! When I said "Oh God" just now, I meant in a, 'Oh help me, Lord', kind of way, not in a cursing sort of way.

Kurt: So you *do* believe in God?

Andy: Err...

Kurt: If you were asking God for help then you must believe in Him; you must believe He exists.

Andy: Oh Go..........sh.

Kurt: I hope you're not trying to mislead me, Mister Reardon. What you say during the course of this interview could have a real bearing on what happens to you in the future. You need to tread carefully.

Andy: I'm not trying to mislead you. It's just ...Let's just skip the Ten Commandments, shall we? I have to admit that I only know a couple of them. Thou shalt not kill, thou shalt not steal and isn't there one about covering your neighbours ox...or something like that?

Kurt writes more notes.

Andy: What's that you're writing?

Kurt: Do you believe Jesus suffered on the cross?

Andy: It can't have been pleasant.

Kurt: How have you benefited from His suffering?

Andy: I don't know.

Kurt: How has the world benefited from His suffering?

Andy: I don't know.

Kurt: Do you think therefore, He sacrificed His life in vain?

Andy: Err...I don't know.

Kurt: You don't seem to know a lot, Mister Reardon. Are you trying to avoid saying something you think might get you into trouble?

Andy: It's not really that. I'm not a very religious person. I have to tell you, this has been a very trying day for me. I mean, last night I was relaxing at home with a cup of cocoa and enjoying 'Free Willy'... on DVD. I went to bed and the next thing I know some strange woman is in bed with me, banging on about The Grim Reaper. Bottom line is...I'm supposed to be dead! I mean, it's a lot to take in.

Kurt: Which religious group do you belong to, Buddhist, Muslim, Methodist, Mormon, Jehovah's Witness, Catholic, C of E? Or are you one of those tiresome people who put 'Jedi' down on application forms.

Andy: As I said, I'm not very religious.

Kurt: Not *very* religious.

Andy: I don't belong to *any* religious group.

Kurt: Why not?

Andy: None of them ever made me feel I *wanted* to belong to them.

Kurt: What is wrong with you? Did you never feel you wanted to be part of a body of likeminded people?

Andy: I get that with my mates at The Legion.

Kurt: And which God do you and your 'mates at The Legion' worship?

Andy: Well, we don't tend to discuss that kind of thing.

Kurt: Do you and your 'mates at The Legion' ever hold pagan rituals in the woods, where you dance naked round a fire and bite the heads of chickens?

Andy: Of course not! We'd never dream of doing anything like that.

Kurt: So, just what *do* you and your friends do?

Andy: Well, for the most part, we play games.

Kurt: Are you playing games with me, Mister Reardon?

Andy: No, of course not!

Kurt: Because, if you are, I strongly advise you to cease from doing so.

Andy: *(A little anxious)* Why would I do that?

Kurt: Are you an atheist?

Andy: No.

Kurt: Are you agnostic?

Andy: I don't know.

Kurt: Just what *do* you believe in?

Andy: I just believe in living as good a life as I can. I don't believe in violence or war. I'd like to think I'm a good person who would help the next man if he needed a hand. That's it really.

Kurt: How much money have you given to charitable organisations over the years?

Andy: I've no idea…some.

Kurt: More than a million?

Andy: You're joking!

Kurt: More than a hundred thousand?

Andy: Not *that* much!

Kurt: How much?

Andy: A few quid here and there.

Kurt: How much?

Andy: *(Getting annoyed)* I DON'T KNOW! Look, do most people know how much they've given to charity or how many flies they've killed? I doubt it.

Kurt: You're not going to help yourself if you lose your temper, Mister Reardon.

Andy: I'm sorry.

Kurt makes more notes.

Kurt: How much harm have you done to the planet?

Andy: What? With aerosols and stuff, you mean?

Kurt: Do you own a car?

Andy: Yes.

Kurt: Do you fly?

Andy: Not personally.

Kurt: I mean by plane?

Andy: I've been on holidays. How else are you supposed to get to Corfu?

Kurt: Have you damaged the ozone layer?

Andy: Not on purpose.

Kurt: Have you ever performed sex with an animal against its wishes?

Andy: NO!

Kurt: Why did you find it necessary to get married three times?

Andy: I didn't *want* to marry three times, but my wives died.

Kurt: *All* of them?

Andy: Yes.

Kurt: This is an unusual situation. How do you account for it?

Andy: I don't know. I suppose I was unlucky. My wives died; all of them in different ways.

Kurt: In light of what has happened now…how do you feel about your wives and what you have to face?

Andy: I'm sorry, I don't understand the question.

Kurt presses on.

Kurt: What contribution did you make to the world?

Andy: I made a few people smile.

Kurt: Is that all?

Andy: I've touched a few people's lives, I think. I had family and friends who loved me and I loved them.

Kurt: Are you a leader or a follower?

Andy: I suppose I'm more of a follower, if I'm honest.

Kurt writes another note and puts what he has written into a folder. Pause.

Kurt: Well, Mister Reardon, it is my belief, following this brief interview, that you are a weak minded, dishonest, vague, argumentative, aggressive person, with no apparent regard for the planet or many of the life forms that inhabit it. You clearly have no real beliefs or opinions, apart from possibly homophobia. I'm going to be hard pressed to highlight any good points. What do you have to say about that, Mister Reardon?

Andy: I don't know what to say. I don't think I'm the person you describe but I don't know the rules or how things are judged here. What can I say?

Kurt: Do you believe there are such things as Heaven and Hell?

Andy: Oh crikey! That sounds like an ominous question.

Kurt: Do you?

Andy: I don't know, but I've got a feeling I'm going to find out.

Kurt: No further questions.

Kurt gets up.

Kurt: Someone will be with you in a moment.

Kurt heads to the door with his file.

Andy: *(Getting out of his chair)* Where are you going?

Kurt: *(Coldly)* Thank you for your co-operation.

Kurt leaves the room.

Andy: What's going to happen to me?

Andy is left alone. He looks at his 'Horny Devil' toy.

Andy: Oh my God… this is it! I'm going to Hell! What a way to end up. If there is a God, I'm sorry if I let you down. I hope this is like 'A Christmas Carol' and I wake up on Christmas morning with a new lease of life and a cheerful disposition. May the Lord have mercy on my soul!

Music: *'Fire' by The Crazy World of Arthur Brown'.*

Blackout.

ACT ONE
Scene Four

An ordinary living room. It has a settee with two armchairs and other bits of furniture scattered around. On the wall there is a portrait of Adolph Hitler in full military uniform next to a picture of 'The Virgin Mary'. On another wall is a large, framed black and white photograph of Angelina Jolie. When the curtain opens Adolph Hitler is stage right, ironing. Jesus Christ is sitting on the settee reading 'The Woodworker'. Hitler is singing 'Delilah'.

Hitler: *(Singing)* My my my, Delilah…Vhy vhy vhy, Delilah…so before ve come to BREAK DOWN ZE DOOR. Forgive me Delilah….

Jesus looks up from reading the magazine.

Jesus: Will you stop that, please?

Hitler: Vot?

Jesus: I'm trying to read.

Hitler: I'm not stopping you.

Jesus: I can't concentrate with you singing that ridiculous song.

Hitler: You don't have to listen if you don't like it. I bet you vouldn't complain if I sang 'Jesus Christ Superstar'.

Jesus: It wouldn't make any difference. I want to

read in peace, that's all. It wouldn't matter if you were singing 'Smack my Bitch Up' or 'Fool If You Think It's Over', I just want some quiet.

Hitler: I like to sing ven I do ze ironing. It makes ze whole thing go a lot qvicker. I hate ironing; I can never do a decent job of ze sleeves.

Jesus: You're terrible at most things, let's face it. It's a nightmare when you're on housekeeping duties. Plus, all you do is complain.

Hitler: Shut up 'Mister High unt Mighty'.

Jesus: Shut up yourself.

Hitler: You think you're so perfect.

Jesus: You're in no position to criticise *me*. You're one of the most hated men in the history of the world. I, on the other hand…not to blow my own trumpet… am one of the most worshiped. So put that in your pipe and smoke it, Adolph!

Hitler: Yah, and I can remember a time ven you had a little more humility.

Jesus: Well, it just goes to show what living with you has done to me.

Hitler: It's always easy to blame ozzer people for your own shortcomings.

Jesus: You are just too much.

Hitler: You vant to take a good hard look at yourself.

Jesus: Well, I'll do that while you're cleaning the loo.

Hitler: I'm not cleaning ze loo.

Jesus: Oh, yes you are.

Hitler: Oh no, I'm not!

Jesus: It's your turn.

Hitler: It is *not* my turn.

Jesus: Check the rota if you don't believe me.

Hitler: I vill.

Jesus: And when you do, you'll see that I'm right… as usual!

Hitler lifts up the shirt he has just ironed and holds it up to the light.

Hitler: You see, ze sleeves. I've somehow ironed a crease into zem.

Jesus: *(Getting up and putting down the magazine)* Oh, for Dad's sake! Let me do it.

Hitler: No. I vill do zis again. It vill be perfect!

Jesus: Give me the iron.

Hitler: No!

Jesus: Give me the iron, Adolph.

Hitler: NO!

Jesus: Look, for the last time, give me the freaking iron!

They are now playing a game of tug of war for the iron.

Hitler: Vill you stop zis at once? You vill burn yourself on ze hot iron!

It has turned into quite a tussle.

Jesus: Well, give it to me, you stubborn little jerk.

Suddenly there is a knock on the door. They stop fighting.

Hitler: Who is zis?

Jesus: How should *I* know?

Hitler: Vhy don't you open ze door unt see who it is?

Jesus: Why don't *you*?

Hitler: Turd!

Jesus: You're not going to make me swear.

Hitler: I got you yesterday.

Jesus: I'm not falling for it.

Hitler: Vot voz it you called me?

Jesus: Never mind.

Hitler: I'm going to tell.

Jesus: You can't do that. I have a reputation.

Hitler: So do I.

Jesus: All right, what's it worth?

Hitler: You clean ze loo.

Jesus: No way!

Hitler: As you vish. Now, vot did you call me? Oh, yes... it began viz a C... Vait till I tell Mother Teresa. She's going to be verr disappointed viz you.

Jesus: You wouldn't.

Hitler: I voud.

Jesus looks at Hitler. He sees Hitler is serious.

Hitler: Unt you *know* I voud.

Jesus: *(Beaten)* All right, you win. I'll clean the loo.

Hitler: Ha! Ha! I love to vin.

There is another knock on the door.

Hitler: Aren't you going to get zat?

Jesus: You really are*...*a*...*

Hitler: Vot?

Jesus: Nothing.

Jesus goes to the door.

Hitler: Oh...Jesus?

Jesus: Yes.

Hitler: Ve're running a bit low on ze 'Toilet Duck', you might vant to get a fresh bottle from ze utility room.

Jesus: Whatever.

He opens the door and Andy is standing there with a young woman, Emma. She is a smiley, bubbly, American girl of about thirty.

Emma: Hello boys, how are you?

Jesus: Hello, Emma. We're fine. Do come in.

Emma and Andy step inside. Andy is gob-smacked at the sight of Jesus and Adolph Hitler in the same room with him.

Andy: *Jesus*!

Jesus: That's me!

Hitler gives the Nazi salute. Andy almost responds but stops himself.

Emma: Andy, this is Jesus and Adolph, they're your housemates for the time being. Jesus, Adolph…this is Andy. He's a new arrival. He'll be staying with you for a little while, so, look after him, won't you?

Hitler: Ve vill give it our best shot.

Jesus: Hi, Andy. I'm Jesus of Nazareth…The Son of God.

Hitler: Don't listen to him. He says zat to everyone; it's a load of stuff unt nonsense.

Jesus: Don't listen to him. His problem is; he has no faith.

Hitler: No faith? I just recognise claptrap ven I hear it, zat's all.

Emma: Now boys, let's not get into all that. Andy, would you like to make yourself comfortable?

Andy steps cautiously into the room.

Jesus: Take the weight off your feet.

Andy: *(Sitting down)* Thanks.

Emma: Andy has just had his evaluation and he's passed it with flying colours, didn't you, Andy?

Andy: Yes, much to my surprise, after what that chap said.

Emma: He had Kurt.

Hitler: Say no more.

Jesus: He likes to give people a hard time. He's a pussycat really.

Andy is sitting there with a look of disbelief on his face.

Emma: Are you all right, Andy?

Andy: This is something else! I mean, you're not really trying to tell me that this is Adolph Hitler and Jesus Christ living in the same house?

Hitler: Ze truth is stranger zan ze fiction, yah?

Jesus: It's true! It really is us.

Jesus puts his arm round Adolph and grins. Hitler shrugs him off.

Hitler: Get off!

Emma: Andy needs a few days to get himself settled before he decides what to do about his domestic situation, don't you, Andy?

Andy: Err...yes.

Emma: Perhaps you two 'men of the world' might be able to help Andy make the right choice.

Hitler: Yah, dis is gutt. I haff a lot of experience about zis. Jesus can make ze tea.

Jesus: Who would take advice from you? What did you ever do?

Hitler: May I remind you that my world domination came verr close to succeeding.

Jesus: Rubbish! You were just a megalomaniac with a massive ego, who bit off more than he could chew.

Hitler: Massive ego? Who called himself ze king of ze Jews? Mind you, zat's a bit like calling yourself ze smartest village idiot.

Emma: Please, boys. Let's try and think about Andy and his situation for the moment. He's had a rough time of it, haven't you, Andy?

Jesus gives Hitler the 'peace sign', Hitler responds with a 'V sign'.

Andy: It's not been my favourite day, I'll admit.

Emma: Andy was married three times in his lifetime.

Hitler: My vurd. Vot a cross to bear.

Jesus: Do you mind not using that phrase, please?

Hitler: Ha!.

Emma: They all died!

Jesus: Heavens!

Emma: They are all waiting to see him again.

Hitler: Vot is zis?

Emma: He needs a little TLC from with a couple of guys like you to give him the benefit of your combined wisdom.

Hitler: Yah!

Jesus: He'll be in good hands.

Emma: Well, I've got a million and one things to do. People are dropping like flies, right now. We'd all be working round the clock, if clocks existed. So, I'll leave you three to get acquainted, all right, Andy?

Andy: Yes, thanks.

Emma: See you later, boys.

All: Bye, Emma.

Emma takes the 'Horny Devil' toy from her bag.

Emma: *(Handing it to Andy)* You forgot this.

Andy: *(Slightly embarrassed)* Err...thanks.

Hitler: *(Looking at the toy)* Ah, a man after my own heart.

Jesus looks on disapprovingly. Emma exits.

Jesus: So, are you coming to terms with the 'way of things' here, Andy?

Andy: Well, this afterlife thing is pretty strange. They say we don't actually exist in physical form, yet people here live their lives as if they were physical beings and do normal physical things. I don't really understand that.

Jesus: That's right, Andy. A lot of it is force of habit but none of us actually exist in any form other than as a spirit. Let me give you an example.

Jesus takes a gun out of the drawer and shoots Hitler. Hitler falls to the floor. After a moment he gets up.

Hitler: *(Dusting himself down)* I vish you vouldn't do zat.

Jesus: I was just demonstrating to Andy about life in the afterlife.

Hitler: I vish you could find anozzer vay of demonstrating. Try shooting yourself next time.

Jesus: You see, Andy. We're not physical but we project ourselves as physical forms; it's the way we do things here. Others see us as we see ourselves and we all interact in what appears to be an actual physical existence.

Hitler: But it's not.

Jesus: That's right. Everything you see, everything you feel, everything you do, is a collective projection of the world as we...all of us...see it.

Andy: I see...I think.

Jesus: You'll get used to it.

Pause.

Hitler: So, you had three vives?

Andy: Three vives?

Jesus: He means wives.

Hitler: He knew vot I said. Ve don't need you to translate.

Jesus: *(To Andy)* He's German.

Hitler: Actually, I'm Austrian, get your facts right.

Andy: You say that like I don't know who he is. That's the amazing thing about this...you two! I can't believe it actually *is* you. The most famous person I'd met before today was...Bill Oddie.

Hitler: Vell, ve heff to be somevere, so vhy not here,

yah?

Andy: How did you two...of all people, end up living in the same house? I mean, I can't think of two more different people.

Hitler: Dis is true. You vont to try living vit zis jack-ass.

Andy: You can't talk about Jesus Christ like that!

Hitler: Vhy not? You shut hef heard vot he called me yesterday, he called me a c...

Jesus quickly puts his hand over Hitler's mouth.

Jesus: The reason we are living in the same house is...I took him on as a challenge. I agreed to help in making him a better person. It was the ultimate challenge.

Hitler: Vot nonsense! How could you make *me* a better person? Vot makes *you* such a big shot?

Jesus: Well, not to put too fine a point on it. I am The Son of God.

Hitler: You're always saying zat, I'd like to see some proof.

Jesus: Proof? You know nothing about religion.

Hitler: All ve have is your vord and a few party-pieces. Show me some DNA results unt zen I might believe you. Ven it comes right down to it, you are nothing more zan a celebrity.

Jesus: Don't you dare call me that!

Hitler: *(To Andy)* He hates it ven I call him zat.

Jesus: He should be downstairs by rights. He's not the least bit grateful.

Hitler: You vud like it if I fell to my knees unt kissed your feet.

Jesus: I'm working on you.

Hitler: Yah, unt I'm vorking on *you*. You're not ze sveetness unt light you verr ven I first met you.

Jesus: This is all by the by. We have a guest. I think we should be helping him not arguing between ourselves.

Hitler: Vell, get on vith it, zen.

Jesus: *(To Andy)* So, Andy, what's your story?

Andy: Well, that lady…Emma, told me that this is the afterlife. She said that anyone I knew who has died will be here somewhere, including my three deceased wives. It seems that when you die you wait for your partner here in the afterlife but if you lose one or more partners, it causes complications. My first wife…Mandy, was tragically killed in a freak accident involving a milk float at Wigan Pier just twelve months after we were married. She was only twenty-three at the time…I was heartbroken. It took me years to get anywhere near over it. My second wife…Vicky, I met when I was thirty-two. We were together for over fifteen years. She died during complications following minor surgery. I couldn't believe it had happened to me again. Vicky was forty-seven. We had two children and a very settled life. The children got me through that one. My third wife, Kerry, died fairly recently after a long battle with cancer...she was seventy one. Now I'm told they're all here waiting for me. I don't know what to do. How can I make a choice like that? I mean, I loved them all. I *married* them all. I didn't expect one day I was going to have to choose who I loved the most.

Hitler: I heff heard of ze luff triangle, not ze luff square.

Jesus: This is going to be a very difficult decision, Andy.

Andy: Don't I know it?

Hitler: Vitch von did you luff ze most?

Andy: That's an impossible question to answer.

Hitler: Nothing is impossible! You must decide vitch von is ze best, unt ditch ze rest!

Jesus: That's typical of what I've come to expect from you. These are women he's loved his whole life. He can't just 'ditch zem', as you put it.

Hitler: Vell, vot else can he do? Zis is no time for sentiment. You must check out ze goods unt make a purchase...it's zat simple!

Jesus: Who....do you think you are kidding, Mister Hitler? *(Jesus laughs)*

Hitler: Oh, verr funny. *(To Andy)* He likes to say zis. He thinks it is amusing. From ze song, yah?

Andy: Yes, I know it.

Jesus: I'm sorry, Andy, this is no time for jokes. We have to help you do the right thing. I think what you need to do is, meet up with each of your three wives here in this house and see what your heart tells you. When you see your first wife again your feelings might have changed. What you need to decide is...who is your true soul-mate?

Hitler: Das is das.

Andy: Is there such a thing?

Jesus: You will know when you have met each of the three of them. Adolph and I will make ourselves scarce while you entertain your three spouses.

Andy: What about you two? Who are your soul mates?

Hitler: Vell, for me it is Eva. She is still downstairs. As for him, he never really met ze right girl but he has a thing for ze Angelina Jolie. He's vaiting for her to die.

Jesus: No, I'm not!

Hitler: Don't let him fool you. Ven she turns up her toes, he'll probably go and collect her himself.

Jesus: You don't know what you're talking about.

Hitler: Zen vhy hef you gone red?

Jesus: *(Embarrassed)* I've not!

Hitler: Ha! Ha! You are *so* transparent!

Jesus: Anyway, like I said, we'll get out of the way. Just tell us when and we'll disappear.

Hitler: Ya, and if you vant to do ze upstairs thing, zat is ok.

Jesus: Oh, please!

Hitler: Vot? Zis is verr important thing. He vill need to know about ze upstairs unt ze downstairs, if you know vot I mean.

Jesus: You don't get any better, do you?

Hitler: If you vere a real man instead of putting yourself on zis high pedestal, you might understand vhy Andy will need to do ze business, yah?

Andy: I think I'll just meet up with them and see what happens, eh?

Hitler: Yah, zis is gutt. As long as you clean your tackle to be on ze safe side.

Jesus: Oh, Adolph!

Andy: Blimey O'Reiley. Yesterday the only things I needed to worry about were how to stop the birds from eating the strawberries on my allotment and how to apply suppositories. Now I'm faced with death, and the most perplexing dilemma that any man could face...choosing between the three great loves of his life, who to spend eternity with, and having to break the hearts of the other two in the process, and as if that wasn't strange enough, I'm being given advice by Jesus of Nazareth and Adolph

Hitler. Edgar would never believe it!

Blackout. Music: *'Heaven Knows I'm Miserable Now' by 'The Smiths.*

ACT TWO
Scene One

Music: *'Three Steps To Heaven' by 'Eddie Cochran'.*

The same room as previous scene. Andy is combing his hair and preening himself in the mirror. Hitler is reading a copy of 'Nuts' magazine. Andy takes a step back and looks at himself in the mirror. He turns to face Hitler.

Hitler: *(Looking goggle-eyed at the magazine)* My vord! I bet she vouldn't need a life jacket if ze ship vent down.

Andy: How do I look, Fuehrer?

Hitler: *(Putting down the magazine)* Yah, you look gutt. Your vife vill be impressed, I'm sure.

Andy: This is such a weird feeling. I haven't seen Mandy for over forty years. I can't believe in the next few minutes she's going to walk through that door. I'm as nervous as a kitten.

Andy starts pacing the room.

Hitler: Don't be nervous. As a man you must be strong. Show her who is ze boss unt who is in ze driving seat.

Andy: *(Looking at his watch)* I keep looking at my watch, then I realise it doesn't work anymore. It's what you would normally do when you're nervously waiting for a date. Oh, Lord... a date...it's not a date.

It's my wife! The wife who died in 1969! This *can't* be happening!

Hitler: Try to stay calm. Ve'll be out of here shortly, just as soon as ze Jew boy has stopped preening himself in zhere.

Hitler gets up and taps on the bedroom door.

Hitler: Hey, Messiah! Are you nearly ready? Zis boy is vearing out ze carpet in here. *(He turns to Andy)* Actually, he's not ze Messiah; he's a verr naughty boy. *(He laughs at his own joke).*

Jesus steps into the room wearing a crown of thorns.

Jesus: How do I look? How's my hair looking? I've tried some different conditioner.

Hitler: You look ze same as you always look. Vhy are you vearing ze robes unt ze crown of thorns again? Can't you ever vear anything else?

Jesus: People expect it. You can't expect The Son of God to go out wearing a baseball cap, Hawaiian shirt and Nike trainers.

Hitler: *(To Andy)* Ze real reason is, no one recognises him unless he vears ze robes. Zhey sink he's just a man viz a beard. His ego can't take it venn people are not fawning all over him.

Jesus: You're no different. When was the last time you went out in anything other than your Nazi uniform?

Hitler: Not zat long ago, zat party Ivan ze Terrible threw. I vent as Sylvester ze cat.

Jesus: That doesn't count. It was fancy dress.

Hitler: Vell, at least I made an effort. You vent as yourself.

Jesus: So?

Hitler: *(To Andy)* It voz amusing. Everybody vanted to know who ze man viz ze beard in ze Jesus costume voz.

Jesus: Never mind that. Are you ready or not? We need to be out of here before Andy's wife arrives.

Hitler: I've been ready for ages. I've been vaiting for you to stop faffing around in zhere.

Jesus: Well, I'm ready. So, let's go.

Hitler: Yah. Let's go!

Hitler slaps Jesus on the back. When he removes his hand it is clear he has stuck a piece of paper with a swastika on Jesus' back.

Hitler: *(Winks at Andy)* Come on zen, old friend, let's paint ze town.

Jesus: Good luck, Andy and don't worry. I'm sure everything will go swimmingly.

They exit through the front door. Andy is left alone. He delivers his speech to the audience.

Andy: Well, what a situation! Mandy! Gosh... I suppose first love never dies; no matter what happens to you or who you meet later on. Has she been waiting for me all this time? If she has been waiting for me, how's she going to feel if I chose Vicky or Kerry? It's going to be nice to see her, though. I know it's a long time ago and I'm probably remembering it with rose tinted spectacles but I have to admit to myself that my brief time with Mandy was probably the happiest time of my life. I always said she was 'The One'. I never admitted that to any of my other wives; or anyone else for that matter. She was a real English rose. Now I have a second chance but this situation is……

Suddenly there is a knock on the door. Andy jumps in surprise.

Andy: Oh, my God! That's her! That's Mandy! I don't think I've ever been as nervous in my life…I mean death. Ah, well, here goes.

Andy goes to the door and opens it. Mandy is standing outside. She is a blonde in her early t wenties. She is a pretty girl but dressed rather like a street hooker in a bright red outfit. She is chewing gum, heavily made up and wearing fishnets. Andy stands there dumbfounded.

Mandy: Well, are you going to ask me in or am I going to stand here like a lemon all day?

Andy: Yes, please come in, Mandy. My God! I can't believe it's you! *Is* it you?

Mandy: *(Striding into the room)* It's me all right. Who the hell are you? I came here to be reunited with me husband. Not to do charity work for 'help the friggin aged'.

Andy: Err...Mandy, it's me!

Mandy: You what!

Andy: It's Andy!

She looks Andy up and down. He is staring at her, his mouth agape.

Mandy: Gordon Bennett! What happened to *you*? You're an old man!

Andy: Well, it's been a long time... more than forty years.

Mandy: We'll have to do something about that. I can't live with you looking like *that*.

Andy: What do you mean, 'do something about it'? This is the way I look.

Mandy: Well, I don't like it! You don't expect me to make the 'two backed beast' with you looking like Old Man Steptoe. You used to turn my head, now you're more likely to turn my stomach.

Andy: Mandy...you've changed! What's happened to you?

Mandy: *I've* changed! Talk about the pot calling the kettle black.

Mandy sits down on the settee, legs akimbo.

Andy: I don't mean you *look* different. I mean you *are* different. You're not anything like I remember. What happened to my English rose?

Mandy: *(Ignoring him)* Hey, you're not going to believe what I just saw? Jesus Christ walking down the road with a swastika on his back. He was with Adolph Hitler. They were looking all chummy. Can you believe it?

Andy: Yes, I know, they're my housemates. Look, that doesn't matter; you've not answered my question.

Mandy: You're sharing a house with *them*...wicked!

She gets up and walks around. She goes into the kitchen, which is off stage.

Andy: Mandy, will you please come in here and talk to me.

Mandy: *(Off)* Only a small kitchen, innit? Are we supposed to be living here, or what?

She comes back into the room.

Andy: Err...I don't know...look, Mandy...I...

Mandy: Where's the bedroom?

Andy points. She walks over and opens the door of the' bedroom and steps inside.

Mandy: I suppose this is Hitler's room, with the swastika wallpaper?

Andy: Well, that's Jesus and Adolph's room.

Mandy: What Hitler and Jesus sleep together? That's just weird.

Andy: Well, they do but only in the Morecambe and Wise sense.

She comes back into the room and faces Andy. She grabs his tie.

Mandy: Listen, Buster, you need to concentrate.

Andy: I beg your pardon.

Mandy: You don't have to look the way you look *now*. As long as you look like yourself, it's OK. Have they not explained it to ya?

Andy: No. I don't know what you're talking about. What did *that* mean?

Mandy: Were not bodies; we're *spirits* of who we are. So, all you have to do is imagine that you look like you did forty years ago and it'll happen...simple as that! They call it projecting. So, get working on it, lover.

Andy: You mean, I can look like I did when I was twenty just by *thinking* that I do.

Mandy: You catch on fast. So, get on it! I want some action! I've waited forty years for this and I'll have you know, I've gone to a lot of trouble for you. I'm wearing some mind-blowing sexy underwear under here that you are *not* going to believe. Just concentrate and we can be 'at it' whenever you're ready.

Andy: Well, I'll try, but don't you think we ought to get to know each other again before we…you know… before we do anything…err…else.

Mandy: You won't say that when you see my panties. *(She gives him a wink)*

Andy: I'm sure they're very nice but…I mean…this is an unusual situation, to say the least. I think I might need a little time to prepare myself mentally for anything other than tea and biscuits and a nice little chat.

Mandy: Are you for real? Listen, Buster, I've been building up for this, you know, I was going to perform fellatio on you.

Andy: Oh Mandy, surely you remember I don't like Spanish music.

Mandy: You what?

Andy: Look, Mandy, I'm a bit nervous, and to be frank, you're not quite what I was expecting. My Mandy was…how can I put it? A shade less boisterous than you appear to be. A little more... gentle...refined...delicate...

Mandy: Oh, get with the programme! That was a long time ago. I'm still your wife, that's the bottom line here. Now, I want you to concentrate on 1969. Remember what you looked like in 1969 and just close your eyes and think of that. Imagine an old photo of yourself from those days. Are you doing that?

Andy has his eyes closed tightly and is concentrating. Music and lighting change.

Andy: I'm trying. 1969. Yes. I wasn't a bad looking chap, was I? I can see myself in my mind's eye. I'm concentrating as hard as I can. 1969, I had a lot more hair and it was dark and wavy.

Mandy: That's right...you were actually quite fit!

Andy opens his eyes.

Andy: Has it worked?

Mandy: No. you're not trying hard enough. You can do it. It's what all the 'wrinklies' do when they get here. So, come on. I want some action between the sheets. I want to play 'hide the sausage'.

Andy: I wish you'd stop saying things like that! You're putting me under pressure and it's hard enough as it is. I'll have another go. Just don't push me.

Mandy: They're red!

Andy: What are?

Mandy: My panties!

Andy: Blood and sand!

Mandy: So, come on, and then you can see for yourself.

Andy: You seem to be rather preoccupied with the notion of having carnal knowledge. I mean, I like a 'roll in the hay' as much as the next man but don't we have rather more pressing matters to consider? Is it not fair to say that the rest of eternity does in fact supercede your libido when push comes to shove in the great scheme of things?

Mandy: You what? Look, never mind the waffle. Get concentrating. We can do as much chatting as you like once you've given me a good seeing to.

Andy: Oh Lord!

Mandy: Get on with it!

Andy: *(Screwing up his eyes)* I'm trying!

Mandy: You can do it!

Andy: 1969…I'm trying as hard as I can…

He opens his eyes again.

Andy: Has it worked this time?

Mandy: No. This is doing my head in! I want to 'get down and dirty' and you're just not trying hard enough. If you think I'm going to live with you looking like that, you can think again! You look like one of the cast of 'Cocoon'.

Andy: Listen, Mandy, that's what we need to discuss; it's not cut and dried by any means. That's why I wanted to see you again. To see what it was like and how I felt about you after all this time. I mean...what about my other two wives? I've not seen them yet.

Mandy slaps Andy across the face.

Mandy: *(Livid)* YOU WHAT! You married someone else? *Two* other someone else's? You slimy git! I thought you and me were forever. Now you turn round and tell me you went off and married some other tart...*two* other tarts...I can't believe what I'm hearing. I thought we were the real deal. I thought you were special!

Mandy starts to cry.

Andy: Look, Mandy, I'm sorry! Please don't cry. It was a long time after you'd gone. I was heartbroken when you died, I've never been able to go anywhere near Wigan Pier since. I was in total despair. What could I do? I was only twenty three when I lost you. I couldn't live my life alone. You have to understand.

Mandy: Oh, I understand all right. You were in such despair that you went off and married someone else. What a sham our wedding was. What a sham our love was!

Andy: It wasn't a sham! I loved you as much as any man could love a woman but I had to accept that life goes on and that's what I ultimately did face. I never believed in the afterlife; I didn't think I'd see you again. This has been a shock to the system, I can tell you.

Mandy: *(Composing herself)* All right. I didn't expect you'd have done what you did but if you can get your act together, I *might* forgive you. What's done is done and we need to get back on track. You married me first, so I get first refusal. That's fair, in't it?

Andy: I can't make a decision like that until I've seen my other two wives. I'm sorry, Mandy, you have to understand that.

Mandy: You need to get yourself sorted. I've been waiting a long time for you you know? Think about that, lover.

Andy: I'm really sorry about that, Mandy. I imagined you were at peace. Not in this place. I don't know what you've been through this last forty odd years but you've changed beyond all recognition. Where's the girl who used to like Terrence Rattigan and played Bach on the recorder? When you died it was like someone sucked the colour out of the sky. I carried on and lived my life but I never felt about anyone the way I felt about you. That's the simple truth.

Mandy: Right! So what are ya dithering for then? Tell those other two tarts to sling their hooks!

Andy: You see, that's the problem…right there! My Mandy would *never* have said something like that.

When we made love we did it to the strains of Rachmaninov...it was magical. Never once did you use an expression like 'Make the two backed beast', or 'hide the sausage'. You are *not* '*my* Mandy'. You are not the person I fell in love with.

He walks up to her and puts his hands to the side of her face and looks her in the eyes.

Andy: I know you're in there somewhere. I know *my* Mandy is in there somewhere.

Mandy: What *are* you on about? You don't half talk a load of crap! Get it together, will ya? And get that face and body of yours sorted. It's not like I'm asking you to go to the gym. Just use your mind, if you've got one!

She walks to the door and opens it.

Mandy: I'll be in touch.

Mandy exits.

Andy: Mandy, wait! Mandy!

She has gone.

Andy: Blood and sand! My English rose! They say that every rose has its thorns, well; I think I just got pricked!

Blackout.

ACT TWO
Scene Two

Music: *'Stairway to Heaven' by 'Led Zeppelin' merging into the 'Coronation Street' theme.*

The same room. Andy is sitting on the settee with Hitler and Jesus. Jesus is knitting. As the scene begins, the closing credits of 'Coronation Street' are heard. Hitler turns the TV off with a remote control.

Hitler: Zat voz not ze best episode I've seen. Zey are running out of ideas, yah?

Jesus: I can take it or leave it these days. I preferred it when Hilda Ogden and Eddie Yates were in it.

Hitler: Yah, unt Alan Bradley got hit by ze tram. Vot do you say Andy? Do you like ze 'Corrie' now viz all ze bimbos? Or are you more off an Ena Sharples man?

Andy: *(Distracted)* Sorry, what did you say, Fuhrer?

Jesus What's up, Andy? Are you worried about Vicky coming round? Is that what's preying on your mind?

Andy: After my last experience, who wouldn't be? Mandy had turned into something unrecognisable. All she wanted to do was jump on my bones. We'd only just been reintroduced a matter of moments and she was talking about performing fellatio.

Jesus: Hmm, seems a peculiar time to be reciting Shakespeare.

Andy: I got the feeling if she had got what she wanted, she'd have bitten off my head, like a praying mantis!

Hitler: She had probably been a long time viz ze wrong people. Zey try to put people together to improve each ozzer but sometimes in vorks ze ozzer vay.

Jesus: Yes, look at us!

Hitler: Ven Bernard Manning arrived they put him vit Gandhi. Vithin no time at all, Gandhi voz telling racist unt sexist jokes. You never know how zeese things pan out.

Andy: Vicky was very set in her ways; she was a lot older. I'm confident she wouldn't be swayed by a 'racist' comedian.

Hitler: Yah. She voz her own voman, yah?

Andy: Yah…I mean, yes.

There is a knock on the door.

Andy: My God! Surely that can't be her. I'm not expecting her for a while yet. They said, after 'Downton Abbey'.

Jesus: Don't worry, Andy. We'll slip out the back way. Come on, Adolph.

Hitler: Dis is dis. To ze batmobile!

They both scurry off through the kitchen. Andy gets

to his feet and composes himself. He walks purposefully to the door and opens it. A man of about fifty with a beard and a navy blue blazer and bright blue shirt and tie is standing there. He is Victor.

Andy: Oh! Hello. Sorry, I was expecting someone else. Are you here for Mister Hitler or Mister Christ? Only you've just missed them.

Victor: No, it's you I came to see, Andy. May I come in?

Andy: Well, it's not really a convenient time, to tell you the truth. You see, I'm expecting a very important visitor anytime now. Maybe we can do this another time.

Victor: Is it about your wife Vicky?

Andy: Yes. How do you know that? And how do you know *my* name? Has something happened to her? Is she not coming?

Victor: If I can come in for just a minute, I can explain.

Andy: Oh, all right, then, but if she turns up I'll need to see her straight away. You see, it's a very important matter.

Victor: I understand.

Victor enters the room and looks around.

Victor: Temporary accommodation, this, is it?

Andy: I don't honestly know. I've not been dead long. I'm in a kind of transitional period, if you like. It's a bit complicated.

Victor: I see.

Victor is standing there looking at Andy. There is an uncomfortable pause.

Andy: Now, what is it I can do for you?

Victor: It's good to see you.

Andy: Err…yes.

Victor: You're looking good.

Andy: Thanks.

Victor takes a step up to Andy, there is a slight pause, he then suddenly throws his arms round Andy. Andy struggles to free himself from Victor's clutches.

Andy: What in tarnation are you doing?

Victor: Andy. Oh, Andy! It's *so* good to see you.

Victor is sobbing. Andy manages to free himself during the next exchange.

Andy: What the Devil is all this about? Who are you, and why in God's name are you getting so upset?

Victor: *(Sitting down, still very emotional)* I'm so sorry! Do you have a Kleenex or a tissue of some kind, please?

Andy takes a hankie from his pocket and hands it to Victor.

Andy: Here.

Victor: *(Blowing his nose into the tissue)* Thank you. (He sniffs) I can't imagine what you must think of me.

Andy: I don't really have an opinion. I mean, you're obviously upset about something, but that's really none of my business. Now, can you tell me who you are and what you know about me and my wife Vicky?

Victor: *(Suddenly singing)* I just called to say I love you; I just called to say how much I care. I just called......

Andy: *(Interrupting)* Please stop that!

Victor: Do you remember that song?

Andy: Yes, I remember it, but to be frank, I find it a bit mawkish for my tastes.

Victor starts to cry again.

Andy: Please stop crying! This is a very uncomfortable situation for me. I can't handle raw emotions at the best of times, but men crying, and a man I don't even know, is significantly worse. Please try and pull yourself together. Be a man!

Victor sobs even louder.

Andy: Blood and sand! Look, my dead wife is going to be here in a minute. How's this going to look to her with you sobbing uncontrollably like this? I mean, I haven't seen her for fifteen years and the moment could potentially be ruined if you can't collect yourself.

Victor: *(Regaining some composure)* I'm so sorry. I wanted this be so special. I'm such a silly sausage.

Andy: Well, that's one way of describing you.

Victor: I'm sorry.

Andy: Are you all right now?

Victor: I think so, yes.

Andy: I'm delighted to hear it.

Victor: Can we start again and pretend I've just arrived?

Andy: I'd rather pretend you were leaving, except without the pretend part.

Victor: That's not a very nice thing to say...to your wife.

Pause.

Andy: *(Dumbstruck)* What?

Victor stands up and looks at Andy.

Victor: Do you not recognise me?

Andy: ...

Victor: Andy, it's me!

Andy: Me?

Victor: Yes.

Andy: You mean...?

Victor: Yes.

Andy: Vicky?

Victor: Yes...well...no...well...sort of.

Andy: Come again?

Victor: Victor.

Andy: Victor?

Victor: Yes.

Andy: Victor. Not Vicky?

Victor: Yes.

Andy: Oh, my God!

Victor: Yes.

Andy: Please tell me this isn't happening.

Victor: It *is* happening.

Andy: That's what I thought.

Victor: I realise this must be a bit of a shock for you.

Andy: *(Flabbergasted)* Oh, not at all! This is just what I should have expected really. I mean, you're a bloke...great! What a nice surprise! My ex-wife... well, dead ex-wife, is a chap called Victor. Do you smoke a pipe? I can smell pipe tobacco. I just don't know what to say. This really caps it all. I think I've lost the will to live and I'm not even alive.

Victor: I'm sorry, Andy.

Andy: No, think nothing of it. You're a bloke...that's fine! A lot of my best friends are blokes; Just, not a lot of my wives.

Victor: Look, Andy, it doesn't have to make a difference, you know.

Andy: What?

Victor: Me being me.

Andy: What do you mean?

Victor: I'm still the person you married.

Andy: I beg to differ. The person I married did *not* have a beard...that much I *do* remember.

Victor: Oh, forget the beard, it's not important.

Andy: I think the beard *is* important, actually. Having said that, if you didn't have it, you'd still be a bloke, just one without a beard.

Victor: This has been a shock to you, I can see that. You might need a little time to chew this over and digest it.

Andy: No amount of chewing or digesting is going to make this any easier to swallow.

Victor: I'm sorry you feel that way, Andy.

Andy: Why on earth do you look like a man? How can you look like a man when you were a woman in life? It makes no sense. We were together fifteen years and you never once gave me the impression that you were unhappy as a woman. You were as feminine as any woman I knew. You had two children and if I remember rightly…you breast-fed. You hated cricket and you used to laugh at Victoria Wood. I mean, when did a man ever laugh at Victoria Wood?

Victor: I kept a lot inside, Andy. I never told a living soul about some of my deeper feelings, but when I arrived here, that was how I chose to be. That is how I see myself and how others see me. As I really am! We can be together again but I'm who I am and you must accept that. I can't change!

Andy: I'm not living with a bloke! What do you take me for? I've never been interested in men. I don't even like it when women have tattoo's and supp pints.

Victor But I'm your wife. You should love me for who I *am*, not who you *want* me to be.

Andy: That's all well and good and I'm all for 'live and let live' but this situation is completely unacceptable. I didn't marry a bloke called Victor; I married a girl called Vicky. Do you see the difference?

Victor Yes, of course I do, but I want you to understand that we are all spirits here. That's what it's really all about. As far as I'm concerned you are my partner and I want to spend the rest of eternity with you. If you can put your prejudices to one side and accept me for what I am, then I'll be waiting for you.

Andy: It's not a matter of prejudice; it's a matter of personal taste. My personal taste does not extend to men with beards who smell of pipe tobacco.

Victor: We are all spirits here. We are not physical beings.

Andy: If that's the case, then why am I standing here looking at a man with a beard?

Victor: Because that's the image I'm projecting. The image I *choose* to project.

Andy: Well, can't you try projecting a different one? Sophie Loren, circa 1960 for instance. Or Brigitte Bardot, before she spent too long in the sun and started to look like an old handbag.

Victor: You don't understand! It doesn't work that way. You have to be true to yourself. You have a lot to learn about the afterlife.

Andy: Well, from what I've seen so far it's a pretty terrible place. I was looking forward to seeing you again and look what I find: Henry the Eighth!

Victor: I'm still the person I was. You need to see that, Andy.

Andy shakes his head.

Victor: I love you, Andy. I always have and I always will. That's all that matters, isn't it?

Andy: Well, not quite all, no.

Victor: Are you worried what your friends will think? Is that what's bothering you? I heard about your new friends. I heard that you, Hitler and Jesus are like three peas in a pod.

Andy: They've been very good to me actually, but that's really not the issue here, is it?

Victor: Then, what is?

Andy: Oh, for goodness sake! Why am I being made to feel bad about this? I can't live with you unless you're Vicky. You're not Vicky...you're Victor! As long as that remains the case then it's 'no way, Jose'. Why can't you just be who you *really* are? You were born a woman and that's what you are!

Victor: I'm going to leave you to think about what I've said. I'll give you some time to talk to your friends and mull everything over. I know it's a difficult decision but you need to think about what's really important.

Victor walks to the door. He turns to Andy.

Victor: I'd like to kiss you before I leave. Would you mind that?

Andy: What...kiss me?

Victor: Just in case I never see you again. Just one kiss. Just in case it is goodbye.

Andy: Look, Vicky…I mean Victor. I don't *want* to kiss you. It feels wrong. I know part of you is still the woman I loved, but you look like Brian Blessed and that kind of makes it a tad less appealing.

Victor: Then, at least let me hug you. That's not too much to ask, is it?

Andy: I'm not sure.

Victor: Oh, surely you wouldn't deny me a little hug, for old time's sake.

Andy: *(Still a little unsure)* Well, I suppose a hug will be OK. Yes, all right.

Victor walks towards Andy. Victor throws his arms around Andy and holds him tightly. For a moment, no-one speaks.

Victor: Do you know how long I've waited to hold you in my arms like this?

Andy: Err…

Victor: It feels good, doesn't it?

Andy: Well, it's certainly affectionate, I can see that.

Victor: Oh, Andy, I do hope it can be you and me for all eternity. Imagine that.

Andy I'm trying to.

Andy suddenly pulls away.

Victor: What is it? What's wrong?

Andy: I felt something stirring …down below.

Victor: Me too!

Andy: I meant *you*!! I meant something stirring in *you…I* don't feel a stirring, let me make that quite clear!

Victor: Oh…sorry! Yes, I didn't realise *that* was going to happen. It's just been so long.

Andy: I noticed! Look, Victor, I'll think about what you've said but don't get your hopes up.

Victor walks again to the door. He stops for a moment in the doorway and turns to Andy.

Victor: Remember the good times.

Andy: I will.

Victor: We'll always have Rhyl.

Andy: Err…yes.

Victor: Goodbye, Andy. I hope you change your mind. I'll be waiting.

Victor blows Andy a kiss and exits through the door.

Andy: *(Still shell-shocked)* Yes, goodbye.

Andy faces the audience.

Andy: This is catastrophic! Is this real, or have I tipped over into madness? My first wife is a tart with a bad attitude and my second looks like Captain Haddock from the Tin Tin stories. I thought they said I had passed the evaluation. Surely this is Hell! How could *anything* be worse than this?

Blackout

ACT TWO
Scene Three

Music: *'You'll Never Get to Heaven if you Break my Heart' by 'The Stylistics'*

The room, as before. Jesus is polishing the picture of Angelina Jolie and singing 'Something in the way she moves' The main door opens and Hitler enters, wearing 'comedy breasts'. He is a little worse for drink but not completely wasted.

Hitler: Honey, I'm home!

Jesus turns.

Jesus: Oh, very funny! Where have you been? Have you been out drinking with your mates from The Gestapo again? I've told you they're a bad crowd. Remember what happened last time.

Hitler: I only had von or two. Don't get on my case. Can't a man let his hair down vonce in a vile?

Jesus: You're already in my bad books.

Jesus removes the 'comedy breasts'.

Hitler: Vot haf I done now?

Jesus: You put your red pants in the wash with my robes. You've completely ruined them.

Hitler: Vot, ze pants?

Jesus: No, you cretin…my robes!

Hitler: Are zey zat bad?

Jesus: If you think I'm going to walk down the street in a pink robe, you've got another thing coming.

Hitler: I vas doing ze vites. I did not realise my red pants vere in zhere.

Jesus: I should just do everything myself. It would make things a hell of a lot easier.

Hitler: Ah! You used the 'H' word.

Jesus: Whatever! Listen, I'll do the washing in future and think on…you owe me one.

Hitler: If you say so. Anyway, zhere are more serious things to think about zan your robes. Vhere is our boy?

Jesus: He's lying down in the bedroom. I think he's depressed.

Hitler: Zis is not gutt. His third vife vill be here soon. He needs to get ready for zat, yah?

Jesus: He's very down; I think he's expecting the worst after his last two experiences.

Hitler: Ze afterlife is a strange place. Ve should have varned him how much it can make people change.

Jesus: Yes and the longer they're here, the more they're likely to have changed.

Hitler: Yah.

Jesus: Go get him. Remind him she's on the way.

Hitler goes and taps on the bedroom door.

Hitler: Andy! Are you getting up now? Your vife vill be here soon.

Andy: *(Off. Sounding flat)* I'll be out in a minute.

Hitler: He does not sound verr up.

Jesus: I told you. He's depressed.

Hitler: He needs to get up unt prepare for battle. Von must dust vonself down unt start all over again.

Jesus: Let's just hope he gets lucky this time.

There is a knock on the door

Hitler: Zat must be her. *(Calling)* Andy!

Jesus: What should we do? Shall we make ourselves scarce?

Hitler: No, Andy needs to be here.

Jesus goes up and taps on Andy's door.

Jesus: Andy, Looks like boat number three has just come in. Be positive, love, third time lucky. *(Turning to Hitler)* He's not responding.

Hitler: *(Striding towards the door)* Enough of zis softly, softly approach.

He raps hard on the door.

Hitler: *(In a ranting, Nazi voice)* You vill open zis door AT VONCE! DO YOU HEAR?

Jesus: Oh, he makes me weak at the knees when he talks like that.

The door opens and Andy sheepishly appears. Another knock on the outside door.

Jesus: Come on, love, she's waiting for you.

Andy: I'm sorry, but this is my last throw of the dice.

Hitler: Just grit your teeth unt face ze music.

Andy walks hesitantly towards the door.

Andy: My dad used to say 'hope for the best and prepare for the worst'.

Andy opens the door... a six foot chicken is standing there.

Chicken: Hello. I....

Andy: Blood and sand!

Andy runs back into his bedroom and slams the door shut. Hitler approaches the chicken.

Hitler: Vot in ze name of Bernard Matthews is zis! Please explain yourself!

Chicken: I'm sorry to trouble you; I represent 'square deals for animals in the afterlife'. I have a leaflet here explaining how....

He is about to hand Hitler a leaflet. Jesus steps to the door.

Jesus: You mean...you're not Kerry?

Chicken: No, mate, I'm Roger. Did you know that conditions for animals are terrible here in......

Hitler: *(Butting in)* Never mind all zat! Get out of here before I do sumsing even *I* might regret.

Chicken: But....but...but...but

Hitler: GET OUT!.......... OUT!

Hitler firmly closes the door on the chicken.

Jesus: Well, whatever next! Poor Andy must be in a state of shock. I'd better go see how he is.

Hitler: Yah, Andy may have expected his vife might be foul, but zis is more zan he vould haf bargained for!

Another knock on the door.

Hitler: Donner unt blitzen, zat must be ze real deal. Vot should ve do now?

Jesus: Well, you might as well let her in. Andy's not going to stir now.

Hitler: Yah, ve can maybe vet her first, unt then if she looks like a paltry excuse for a vife ve can send her packing.

Hitler opens the door, Kerry is standing there. She is an attractive redhead in her thirties, dressed from head to toe in white.

Hitler: Yah, dis is gut!

Kerry: Hello, I'm Kerry. Adolph Hitler! What are *you* doing here?

Hitler gives the Nazi salute.

Hitler: I live here.

Kerry: Well, really, you were the last person I expected to see.

Kerry steps into the room. Jesus approaches Kerry.

Jesus: Hello Kerry, I'm Jesus of Nazareth...The Son of God.

Hitler: Oh, here ve go.

Kerry: What a privilege to meet you. You know, I never go anywhere without my crucifix. I wear it always close to my bosom. You are my inspiration.

Jesus: Well, that's very flattering, but that particular experience isn't one I like to relive.

Kerry: *(Singing)* Stand up stand up for Jesus, ye

soldiers of the cross...

Jesus: Enough already.

Kerry: Let me kiss your feet, Lord.

Jesus: Oh, no need to stand on ceremony here.

Kerry: *(Singing)* Praise him, praise him, praise him...

Jesus: Steady the buffs...

Kerry: Your modesty comes as no surprise: Such a divine presence; such humility; such serenity.

Hitler: Such a need for ze sick bag.

Kerry: *(To Hitler)* You should bow before him, Hitler.

Hitler: In his dreams.

Jesus is nodding. Hitler shakes his head.

Kerry: Why, you aren't fit to wipe his bottom. *(Turning to Jesus)* If you'll pardon my even mentioning such a private area of your anatomy, Lord.

Jesus: Well, we're all the same underneath...except that Hitler has only got one ball.

He laughs. Kerry laughs also. Hitler shakes his head.

Hitler: Oh, ze old vons are ze best, yah?

Jesus: If you're wondering about Andy, he's just getting ready; he shouldn't be long, if you'd like to take a seat.

Kerry: Thank you, Lord.

Kerry sits down. Hitler sits next to her, before Jesus can get to the settee.

Jesus: Can I get you something to eat or drink, Kerry?

Kerry: Do you mean to eat of the body and drink the blood of Christ from the Holy Grail in an act of communion?

Jesus: Oh...sounds painful. No, I was thinking more of a nice cup of tea and maybe a Jaffa Cake?

Kerry: In that case, no thank you. I don't eat or drink. It seems pointless to me when you don't need to.

Hitler: Some people say zat but I still enjoy ze sensation of eating. It stirs ze memory unt makes you relive zat experience. I don't know vot I'd do if someone told me I'd never be able to enjoy anozzer bag of ze pickled onion Monster Munch.

Kerry: It's a matter of opinion. I prefer to abstain.

Hitler: Dis is dis. As a spirit I still enjoy many of ze physical pleasures I remember from my time on Earth. I still enjoy going to ze toilet. You can't beat a gutt bowel movement. Some habits are hard to break, yah?

Jesus: Oh, Adolph!

Hitler: Vot?

Embarrassed pause.

Kerry: So, how is my husband?

Jesus: Well, he's had a couple of bad experiences with his two previous spouses, but you seem to be a nice, attractive and well adjusted person. You're not a bloke, you're not a bird...in the feathered sense... and you're not, on the face of it...a slapper, if you'll pardon my terminology.

Kerry: Sorry?

Hitler: He means, you don't look ze sort who 'puts it about'.

Kerry: I certainly hope not. Anyway, I don't *do* sex. There's no point in having a physical relationship when you're not a physical being.

Hitler: I know some people share zat view. For myself, I like to get my end avay at any unt every opportunity; even if it is just in ze mind. Only last veek, I invited two buxom Hungarian girls over to enjoy an evening of Sadomasochism with some new rubber......

Jesus: *(Interrupting)* Please, Adolph! The young lady is not interested in the details of your sordid sex life.

Hitler: I voz just making ze small talk.

Jesus: I agree with you, Kerry. I myself do not indulge in any kind of sexual activity. But I must admit...I do like to tuck into a KFC bargain bucket on occasion.

Hitler: Hang on! Vot about zat party vhen you got 'out of your head' on tequila slammers unt 'had' Princess Diana in ze back bedroom?

Jesus: I didn't 'have her', you moron. I told you at the time, we were merely discussing 'conspiracy theories'.

Hitler: Ve could hear you through ze door. Don't think you can fool me. I've never heard so much screaming since Himmler took up dentistry.

Jesus: Look, shut up, will ya? You really are a.......

Hitler: Vot? Vot am I?

Jesus: *(Looking at Kerry, who is still smiling)* You're someone who needs help. That's what you are. I feel sorry for you.

Hitler: You are such a prat! 'King of kings', vot tosh!

Kerry: *(Interrupting them)* Gentleman, please. I really would like to see my husband, if it's all the same to you.

Jesus: I do apologise. Mister Hitler is a 'bit much' at times, especially when he's been 'on the sauce'. Adolph! Go and get Andy...NOW!

Hitler: *(Going to the bedroom)* I luff it vhen you are masterful.

Hitler taps on Andy's door and goes inside.

Jesus: Well, Kerry, you look like a nice girl to me. I hope you're not going to deliver another blow to our Andy. I don't think he could take another knock. I must say, you're not what I imagined from what Andy said about you but there again, Andy was describing you as a woman in her seventies and you are projecting a much younger image.

Kerry: This is what I looked like when I was in my thirties. I was a confident girl in those days. It was a good time in my life.

Jesus: Well, I hope you've got good news for our Andy. Adolph and I have been really worried about him.

Kerry: They always said, 'it's good to have a friend in Jesus'. It's nice to see that's true.

Kerry touches Jesus' hand. They smile at each other. At that moment Andy and Hitler enter the room. Kerry stands up and she and Andy look at each other for a moment. Kerry takes a step towards Andy. Andy takes a step towards Kerry. They pause for a moment and then throw their arms around each other. Hitler signals to Jesus and they both discreetly exit by the front door. Andy and Kerry break the embrace and take a good hard look at each other.

Andy: It's good to see you, Kerry.

Kerry: It's good to see you too, Andy. I have prayed for you so many times.

Andy: My God, you look gorgeous! I've seen pictures of you looking like this but in the flesh you are simply radiant!

Kerry: Yes but remember, Andy, what you are seeing is not flesh but spirit; the light that my spirit generates here in the afterlife.

Andy: Yes, of course. It's just the way you appear. The afterlife doesn't seem to have done *you* any harm.

Kerry: My collector was so comforting and gentle; he took all my pain away. It was such a relief, in the end, to slip away into the light after all the treatment and those dark days.

Andy: Well, it's nice to see one of my wives isn't a freak. I was beginning to think I was cursed. Seeing you is the first good thing that's happened to me since I got here. Well, apart from meeting my new friends. Jesus is a lovely fella and Adolph isn't as black as he's painted; he's got a heart of gold. He and Jesus wind each other up a bit but they love each other really.

Kerry: It's nice you feel that way about them. Shall we sit down?

They do.

Andy: So, what happens now? You're here and I'm here and-well, where do we *go* from here?

Pause.

Kerry: What are you looking for, Andy?
Andy: What am I looking for?

Kerry: In the afterlife?

Andy: I don't honestly know. They told me I had to make a decision about who I was going to spend eternity with and when I met Mandy and Vicky… I realised I couldn't contemplate spending an afternoon with them…let alone eternity. So, now here we are and you like a breath of fresh air, I mean, I've learnt to expect the unexpected here. For a minute there, I thought you were a giant chicken. I'm delighted to see you're not.

Kerry: A what?

Andy: It doesn't matter...

Kerry: Well, I'm not a chicken…as you can see.

Andy: Indeed not...

Kerry: I was worried about you when I crossed. I thought about you a lot.

Andy: I thought about you, too. I didn't know you were here like this. I never really thought that we existed in spirit. I just believed when you 'popped your clogs' it was 'Goodnight, Vienna!'

Kerry: Andy, I was always a spiritual person, you knew that...and now...I want to do good work here. That's why I'm doing what I'm doing.

Andy: And what is that? What *are* you doing?

Kerry: I'm a collector.

Andy: A collector? Like that dizzy Eva? If you know who she is.

Kerry: Oh yes, we all know Eva.

Pause.

Kerry: Andy, let me ask you a question and please answer it honestly.

Andy: Yes, of course.

Kerry: Would you have chosen me? Was I really 'the love of your life'? Was I 'the one', as they say?

Andy: Well, it's something of an odd scenario, isn't it? I mean, Mandy's a bit 'full on' and Vicky...well...it's the little matter of the 'meat and two veg'.

Kerry: You make it sound like 'Hobson's Choice'...

Andy: I wouldn't have put it like that. You are my wife. How can anyone live in the past? Vicky and Mandy have changed. They're not the people they once were.

Kerry: Neither am I.

Pause.

Kerry: I'm not who I was. I think if we're honest we were never 'in love' in the way that we had been before with other people in our youth. We loved each other but we were more like companions. I care about you, Andy, but I have a job to do. I can help others to come to terms with their passing. It's what I believe I was destined to do. I do hope you understand.

Andy: I wouldn't dream of asking you to spend eternity with me if that was something you didn't want to do. I respect your wishes and understand your reasons. I just hope we can still see each other from time to time. I would like that.

Kerry touches Andy's hand.

Kerry: Yes, of course.

Andy gets up and walks to the window.

Andy: Well, what do you do? I was wondering how I was going to make a choice between the three women I loved and in the end the choice was made for me. I don't know what lessons this has taught me but maybe it will teach me something about not having expectations. If the three women of my life had been the women they were……

There is a knock on the door.

Kerry: Are you expecting anyone?

Andy: No. it can't be Jesus or Adolph. They'll be 'down the club'.

Andy goes to the door.

Kerry: At least you know it's not someone selling life insurance.

Andy opens the door and to his surprise it is Eva. She is dressed in a green fairy outfit, complete with wand.

Eva: Hi.

Andy: Shiver me timbers!

Eva: It's me!

Andy: So I can see.

Eva: Can I come in?

Andy: Do you have to?

Eva: Oh, don't be like that.

Eva walks in and spins around waving her wand.

Eva: Well, you said you didn't believe in fairies...Ta da!

Andy: Err, this is my wife Kerry.

Eva: Hi.

Kerry: Hello Eva.

Pause.

Eva: This is nice, isn't it? Are you two getting reacquainted?

Andy: We *were*.

Eva: That's nice!

She stands there, grinning.

Andy: Eva, I have to tell you that since I met you, things have gone from bad to worse and the sight of you now does not exactly fill me with glee. The only reason I'm not screaming, is that you can't possibly make things any worse than they are. I just know you're here to deliver some cataclysmic news. So, let's just get it over with.

Eva: Oh, yeah, right. Well, what do you want first, the good news or the bad news?

Andy: Oh, crikey. Let's have the bad news. Let's have something I'm used to. Come on; give me your best shot!

Eva: Well, the bad news is…I've just had my bottom smacked.

Andy: Is that supposed to be bad news?

Eva: Well, yeah! *(She snorts)*

Andy: That is the kind of bad news I can handle. What about the good news?

Eva: The good news is, well…it's not entirely good news, because, it's because of the good news that there's bad news, if you know what I mean. It's because of the good news, that I had my bottom smacked, which was of course the bad news, which wouldn't have even happened if there hadn't been the good news in the first place. Actually, when I said I had my bottom smacked, I didn't mean it figuratively. I meant it literally...if that's the right way round.

Andy: Will you please get to the point?

Eva: What *is* the point?

Andy: The good news.

Eva: The good news?

Andy: Yes.

Eva: What good news?

Andy: The good news that you're supposed to pass on to me. *That* good news!

Eva: Sorry. I thought you meant *you* had some good news.

Andy: Will you please just tell me what the good news is, before I explode.

Eva: Oh, right, hang on...I've got it written down.

She pulls out a piece of paper and reads.

Eva: Put Jimmy Saville in with Osama Bin Laden...

They all look at each other confused.

Eva: I think that might be the wrong scrap of paper.

She pulls out another scrap of paper.

Eva: Oh, hang on...this might be it...err...'You're going home'!

Andy: What?
Eva: I'm sorry! it was all my fault! Bit of a faux pas on my part. It seems you shouldn't be here yet...yeah. Got a bit muddled about dates; it's always been a problem of mine. I could never understand how the twentieth century always began with a nineteen. I'm such a dizzy Lizzy.

Andy: You mean, I'm not dead?

Eva: Nope.

Andy: Not even slightly?

Eva: Not even an itsy witsy teeny weenie yellow polka-dot bikini bit dead.

Andy: I don't know what to say…I'm stunned!

Eva: The Grim Reaper himself summoned me in. He wasn't a happy bunny, I can tell you. He told me I have to make absolutely sure I don't make another blunder. I'm to take you back to the exact time I picked you up. I hope I don't make a 'pig's breakfast' of it. I've got it all written down in my little book of 'what's what'. Trouble is, I'm not sure where I left it.

Andy is dancing 'round the room singing a brief chorus of 'Alive and Kicking'.

Andy: I'm going home! I'm not dead! I can't believe it! I'm alive!

Eva: I just need to know *when* to take you back and...Oh yeah. I have to remember to wipe your memory of the afterlife...err... I think that's it...err... was there something else? I got distracted by a hunky fella walking past the window. That was me... gone! *(She snorts)*

Kerry rises and approaches Eva.

Kerry: Listen, Eva, I can see you're a bit stressed out by all of this. I know GR and I know what he'd do if you did make another mistake with this client.

Eva: He'd do his fruit! *(She snorts)*

Kerry: Listen, let me help you out. I know the client's history and I'll make sure I wipe his memory and get him back where he belongs. If you know anything about me, then you'll know I'm the personification of efficiency. Let me take care of it. How does that sound?

Eva: Well, I don't know what personarification of effeminacy is, but if you would, that would be brilliant! Yeah! Hang on...isn't there a rule about not collecting your own?

Kerry: That's true, but I'm not collecting him, I'm *returning* him.

Eva: Oh, yeah. Well, that's OK, then. Yeah. Fantastic!

Kerry: Well, I'll take care of things here. You can relax now. Job done!

Eva: Right.

Eva is still standing there.

Kerry: Thank you Eva, you can go.

Eva: Oh, OK. *(To Andy)* See ya.

Andy: Not too soon, I hope.

Eva exits.

Kerry: Well, it seems you're not dead after all.

Andy: So it would appear.

Kerry: Let's get you home, then.

Andy stops.

Andy: Wait a minute. Some things still don't make sense.

Kerry: Like what?

Andy: If this is the spirit world, then how can I be here if I'm not a spirit? Aren't they all supposed to be projections of how that spirit sees itself?

Kerry: That's correct, but you *are* a spirit. You don't have to be dead to have a spirit. That will also explain why your watch has stopped. Eva picked up your spirit, not your body. Your body is safe and sound, waiting to be reunited with you.

Andy: Are you going to erase my memory?

Kerry: Yes. You won't remember anything about the afterlife. It will just seem like a vaguely remembered dream.

Andy: Gosh!

Kerry: Are you ready to go home?

Andy: I guess so. There is just *one* other thing, though. What about my friends, Adolph and Jesus. I won't get to say goodbye to them.

Kerry: I'll tell them you said 'goodbye'.

Andy: Tell them 'thanks for everything', and tell them to be nice to each other.

Kerry: I will, but don't expect miracles...even from Jesus.

Andy: I won't.

Kerry: I hope things work out for you, Andy. I'll see what I can do. You deserve some good fortune.

Andy: Gosh, I feel quite emotional. I feel like Dorothy in 'The Wizard of Oz'. It's like I've been here forever. It's sort of like time stands still here, isn't it?

Kerry: That's exactly what it is. We can *make* time stand still. You know, Andy... there's so much you could have learned about life and the afterlife. It's so complex and interesting. If you had stayed I'd have explained it to you but maybe another time. Are you ready to face your future, Andy?

Andy: Well, ready as I'll ever be.

Kerry: Remember, you're going to forget all about me, Eva, Hitler, Jesus, giant chickens and everybody else you've met here.

Andy: I understand.

Kerry: *(Taking Andy's hand)* Time to go, Andy.

Blackout

ACT TWO
Scene Four

A bedroom, full of 1960s posters. Someone is under the covers. Kerry is sitting on the bed. She has her hand resting on the covers.

Kerry: Time to wake up, Andy. You're not in Kansas anymore.

A low moan starts to come from under the covers. Andy emerges but he is a young man; in his early twenties.

Andy: Where am I? What happened? *(To Kerry, only half recognising her)* Hello.

Kerry: Hello. You're home.

Andy: Home?

Kerry Have a look.

Andy gets out of bed, still a little bleary. He walks up to the mirror.

Andy: Oh, my God! What... Is that me?

Andy stares at himself then runs around the room picking things up.

Andy: *(at the top of his voice)* It's the sixties! Oh, my God! I'm young! THE SIXTIES!

Kerry: Try to keep your voice down. You'll need

some time to adjust to your new, or rather...old life and surroundings.

Andy: Jesus, this is incredible!

He stops himself.

Andy: Jesus?

Jesus appears in a spot, eating an Easter egg.

Jesus: You rang. Well, I'm a bit jealous; I thought I was the only one who gets resurrected round here.

Andy: It's Jesus!

Jesus: Have a good one, Andy. Hope you enjoy your second bite of the cherry. Adolph's here; he just wanted to say goodbye.

Hitler appears in a spot, eating 'Monster Munch'.

Andy: *(To Kerry)* It's Adolph!

Hitler: Good luck, Andy. I'm just off to meet zhose buxom Hungarian fraulein's at an Ann Summer's party. No rest for ze vicked, eh? Give her von for me...

Jesus: Oh, Adolph.

Hitler makes a crude arm gesture. Andy laughs and smiles. Kerry waves her hand in front of Andy's face. The spots go out.

Kerry: Forget. You must forget it all.

Andy holds his head in his hands. The sound of a female voice singing 'If Paradise is Half as Nice' is heard off. For a moment Andy seems perplexed by this. He looks in the mirror again.

Andy: Is that...?

Kerry: Don't be alarmed, everything's going to be fine. Try not to over-react.

The door opens and Andy leaps in shock. The young Mandy enters. This is the Mandy, Andy had described earlier; the English rose. She is shocked at Andy's reaction.

Mandy: What on Earth's wrong? You nearly jumped out of your skin.

Andy: Mandy? It's...you!

Mandy: Of course it's me. How many more wives have you got?

Andy: *(With a look to Kerry)* You are...'The One'.

Mandy: I'm glad to hear it. And you are '*a* one'... that's for sure. So, how do I look? Do you like my new outfit?

Andy: *(Still stunned)* You look gorgeous. Stunning.

Mandy: I just bought it. I'm meeting Pam.

Andy: Oh, right...Where you meeting her?

Mandy: Your memory! Are you sure you're twenty three and not seventy three? We talked about this... Wigan Pier.

Andy: Wigan Pier?

Mandy: Yes. There's a lovely little French bistro just opened there.

Andy: Oh, my God!

Mandy: What's up?

Andy: *(Suddenly)* I don't want you to go...not there!

Mandy: Why not?

Andy: I...I...don't know...I have an odd feeling about it.

Mandy: Oh, Andy, I told you yesterday I was going. I've been looking forward to it.

Andy: Did you? I mean...oh yeah...you did! But that was *then*...and this is also then... except that 'then' is kind of...'now', so to speak.

Mandy: Sorry?

Andy grabs Mandy by the waist.

Andy: Don't go! I need you.

Mandy: Need me?

Andy: Yes....I need you... I'm feeling...rampant!

Mandy: That's nothing new. You're always feeling

rampant.

Andy: Yes but today I'm feeling extra rampant. Like the most rampant ram in a field of extremely rampant rams.

Mandy: Andy, I promised Pam. I'll be back before you know it and you can be as rampant as you like.

Andy: But you can meet Pam anytime you like... but not today...and not there. I swear on my life I will never ask you to do this again. Pleeaaasssse.

Kerry waves a hand in front of Andy. He collapses on the bed.

Kerry: Good bye, Andy. Have a good life.

Kerry exits .Mandy goes to Andy. Andy suddenly sits up revived. He smiles at Mandy.

Mandy: Are you OK?

Andy: Never felt better.

Mandy: So, what's the problem with me going to Wigan Pier?

Andy: Oh, is that where you're going?

Mandy: Yes, to the French bistro.

Andy: Nice.

Mandy: You really are behaving very oddly. I'm going now, no more arguments, OK?

Andy: OK.

Mandy: *(Surprised at his change)* I'll see you later.

Andy: Enjoy yourself. Love you.

Mandy: Love you too.

She heads to the door, turns to look at Andy. He smiles at her. She shrugs and exits. Andy is left alone. He looks around the room. He goes to the mirror and looks at himself. He looks deep in thought.

Andy: *(Singing quietly)* If paradise is half as nice as heaven that you take me to, who needs paradise I'd rather have...you...*(Andy stops, as if a sudden thought hit him)*

Mandy enters fuming.

Mandy: Some people!

Andy: What's up?

Mandy: You wouldn't credit some people, would you?

Andy: What happened?

Mandy: As I came out, just now, some woman was slashing my tyres right in front of my face. Then she just walked calmly away.

Andy: What did you do?

Mandy: For some reason I just stood there rooted to

the spot. She didn't look the type; attractive, presentable women with striking red hair.

Andy: Gosh!

Mandy: Well, after having vandalised my moped, she then had the good grace to actually apologise... and get this...as she walked away, she turned and said "You'll thank me for it someday".

Andy: She sounds barking!

Mandy You're telling me.

Andy: ...But she was right about one thing.

Mandy: Right about what?

Andy: Well, she stopped you from going out. I did say I had an odd feeling about it.

Mandy: Yes, well, I think we all know about your 'odd feelings', and they usually involve a certain part of your anatomy below the waist.

Andy: If you say so.

Mandy: I do.

Andy: Well, that's frog's legs on Wigan Pier off the menu, I suppose. I'm just trying to think what else a young married couple like us can do in a room like this, with very little furniture, no telly, a broken record player and an ample sized, reasonably robust bed.

Mandy: And what conclusion did you draw?

Andy: That's something I'd like to discuss with you if

you'd like to step this way.

He takes her hand and leads her to the bed.

Mandy: Well, as I now appear to be stranded here with you, I might just have to take what you have to offer.

Andy: Sounds good to me.

Andy takes her in his arms and kisses her.

Andy: You know what, Mand?

Mandy: What?

Andy: It sure is good to be alive.

Mandy: It sure is.

They both collapse on the bed giggling.

THE END

Curtain call music: *'Spirit in the Sky' by Norman Greenbaum.*

Author's Note: The Alternative Ending.

The alternative ending: The ending of the play has always been the tying up of loose ends. Andy's third wife is a relatively straight character, compared with what comes before. When we first produced the play in 2010 it was felt that the comedy went a little flat. For the second production in 2012 I attempted a new ending but that was overwritten and was later scrapped.

In the third production in 2013 I wrote 'the alternative ending' seen here. People seemed to prefer that, as it took the madness of the play a stage further and kept the laughs going. However, for the forth production, Elspeth Fisher (the director) asked me to write a condensed version of the original ending, as she felt the alternative ending 'a bit too much'. So, I rewrote it once again. Opinions are divided; hence, both versions are included here for the reader to decide for themselves.

ALTERNATIVE ENDING

ACT TWO
Scene Three

Music: *'You'll Never Get to Heaven if you Break my Heart' by 'The Stylistics'*

The room, as before. Jesus is polishing the picture of Angelina Jolie and singing 'Something in the way she moves' The main door opens and Hitler enters, wearing 'comedy breasts'. He is a little worse for drink but not completely wasted.

Hitler: Honey, I'm home!

Jesus turns.

Jesus: Oh, very funny! Where have you been? Have you been out drinking with your mates from The Gestapo again? I've told you they're a bad crowd. Remember what happened last time.

Hitler: I only had von or two. Don't get on my case. Can't a man let his hair down vonce in a vile?

Jesus: You're already in my bad books.

Jesus removes the 'comedy breasts'.

Hitler: Vot haf I done now?

Jesus: You put your red pants in the wash with my robes. You've completely ruined them.

Hitler: Vot, ze pants?

Jesus: No, you cretin…my robes!

Hitler: Are zey zat bad?

Jesus If you think I'm going to walk down the street in a pink robe...you've got another thing coming.

Hitler: I vas doing ze vites. I did not realise my red pants vere in zhere.

Jesus: I should just do everything myself. It would make things a hell of a lot easier.

Hitler: Ah! You used the 'H' word.

Jesus: Whatever! Listen, I'll do the washing in future and think on…you owe me one.

Hitler: If you say so. Anyway, zhere are more serious things to think about zan your robes. Vhere is our boy?

Jesus: He's lying down in the bedroom. I think he's depressed.

Hitler: Zis is not gutt. His third vife vill be here soon. He needs to get ready for zat, yah?

Jesus: He's very down; I think he's expecting the worst after his last two experiences.

Hitler: Ze afterlife is a strange place. Ve should have varned him how much it can make people change.

Jesus: Yes and the longer they're here the more they're likely to have changed.

Hitler: Yah.

Jesus: Go get him. Remind him she's on the way.

Hitler goes and taps on the bedroom door.

Hitler: Andy! Are you getting up now? Your vife vill be here soon.

Andy: *(Off. Sounding flat)* I'll be out in a minute.

Hitler: He does not sound verr up.

Jesus: I told you...he's depressed.

Hitler: He needs to get up unt prepare for battle. Von must dust vonself down unt start all over again.

Jesus: Let's just hope he gets lucky this time.

There is a knock on the door

Hitler: Zat must be *her*. *(Calling)* Andy!

Jesus: What should we do? Shall we make ourselves scarce?

Hitler: No, Andy needs to be here.

Jesus goes up and taps on Andy's door.

Jesus: Andy, Looks like boat number three has just come in. Be positive, love, third time lucky. *(Turning to Hitler)* He's not responding.

Hitler: *(Striding towards the door)* Enough of zis

softly, softly approach.

He raps hard on the door.

Hitler: *(In a ranting, Nazi voice)* You vill open zis door AT VONCE! DO YOU HEAR?

Jesus: Oh, he makes me weak at the knees when he talks like that.

The door opens and Andy sheepishly appears. Another knock on the outside door.

Jesus: Come on, love, she's waiting for you.

Andy: I'm sorry, but this is my last throw of the dice.

Hitler: Just grit your teeth unt face ze music.

Andy walks hesitantly towards the door.

Andy: My dad used to say 'hope for the best and prepare for the worst'.

Andy opens the door... a six foot chicken is standing there.

Chicken: Hello. I....

Andy: Blood and sand!

Andy runs back into his bedroom and slams the door shut. Hitler approaches the chicken.

Hitler: Vot in ze name of Bernard Matthews is zis!

Please explain yourself!

Chicken: I'm sorry to trouble you; I represent 'square deals for animals in the afterlife'. I have a leaflet here explaining how....

He is about to hand Hitler a leaflet. Jesus steps to the door.

Jesus: You mean...you're not Kerry?

Chicken: No, mate, I'm Roger. Did you know that conditions for animals are terrible here in......

Hitler: *(Butting in)* Never mind all zat! Get out of here before I do sumsing even *I* might regret.

Chicken: But....but...but...but

Hitler: GET OUT!.......... OUT!

Hitler firmly closes the door on the chicken.

Jesus: Well, whatever next! Poor Andy must be in a state of shock. I'd better go see how he is.

Hitler: Yah, Andy may have expected his vife might be foul, but zis is more zan he vould haf bargained for!

Another knock on the door.

Hitler: Donner unt blitzen, zat must be ze real deal. Vot should ve do now?

Jesus: Well, you might as well let her in. Andy's not

going to stir now.

Hitler: Yah, ve can maybe vet her first, unt then if she looks like a paltry excuse for a vife ve can send her packing.

Hitler opens the door. Kerry is standing there. She is an attractive redhead in her thirties, dressed from head to toe in white.

Hitler: Yah, dis is gut!

Kerry: Hello, I'm Kerry. Adolph Hitler! What are *you* doing here?

Hitler gives the Nazi salute.

Hitler: I live here.

Kerry: Well, really, you were the last person I expected to see.

Kerry steps into the room. Jesus approaches Kerry.

Jesus: Hello Kerry, I'm Jesus of Nazareth…The Son of God.

Hitler: Oh, here ve go.

Kerry: What a privilege to meet you. You know, I never go anywhere without my crucifix. I wear it always close to my bosom. You are my inspiration.

Jesus: Well, that's very flattering, but that particular experience isn't one I like to relive.

Kerry: *(Singing)* Stand up stand up for Jesus, ye soldiers of the cross...

Jesus: Enough already.

Kerry: Let me kiss your feet, Lord.

Jesus: Oh, no need to stand on ceremony here.

Kerry: *(Singing)* Praise him, praise him, praise him...

Jesus: Steady the buffs...

Kerry: Your modesty comes as no surprise: Such a divine presence; such humility; such serenity.

Hitler: Such a need for ze sick bag.

Kerry: *(To Hitler)* You should bow before him, Hitler.

Hitler In his dreams.

Jesus is nodding. Hitler shakes his head.

Kerry: Why, you aren't fit to wipe his bottom. *(Turning to Jesus)* If you'll pardon my even mentioning such a private area of your anatomy, Lord.

Jesus: Well, we're all the same underneath...except that Hitler has only got one ball.

He laughs. Kerry laughs. Hitler shakes his head.

Hitler: Oh, ze old vons are ze best, yah?

Jesus: If you're wondering about Andy, he's just

getting ready; he shouldn't be long, if you'd like to take a seat.

Kerry: Thank you, Lord.

Kerry sits down. Hitler sits next to her, before Jesus can get to the settee.

Jesus: Can I get you something to eat or drink, Kerry?

Kerry: Do you mean to eat of the body and drink the blood of Christ from the Holy Grail in an act of communion?

Jesus: Oh...sounds painful. No, I was thinking more of a nice cup of tea and maybe a Jaffa Cake?

Kerry: In that case, no thank you. I don't eat or drink. It seems pointless to me when you don't need to.

Hitler: Some people say zat but I still enjoy ze sensation of eating. It stirs ze memory unt makes you relive zat experience. I don't know vot I'd do if someone told me I'd never be able to enjoy anozzer bag of ze pickled onion Monster Munch.

Kerry: It's a matter of opinion. I prefer to abstain.

Hitler: Dis is dis. As a spirit I still enjoy many of ze physical pleasures I remember from my time on Earth. I still enjoy going to ze toilet. You can't beat a gutt bowel movement. Some habits are hard to break, yah?

Jesus: Oh, Adolph!

Hitler: Vot?

Embarrassed pause.

Kerry: So, how is my husband?

Jesus: Well, he's had a couple of bad experiences with his two previous spouses, but you seem to be a nice, attractive and well adjusted person. You're not a bloke, you're not a bird…in the feathered sense… and you're not, on the face of it…a slapper, if you'll pardon my terminology.

Kerry: Sorry?

Hitler: He means, you don't look ze sort who 'puts it about'.

Kerry: I certainly hope not. Anyway, I don't *do* sex. There's no point in having a physical relationship when you're not a physical being.

Hitler: I know some people share zat view. For myself, I like to get my end avay at any unt every opportunity; even if it is just in ze mind. Only last veek, I invited two buxom Hungarian girls over to enjoy an evening of Sadomasochism with some new rubber……

Jesus: *(Interrupting)* Please, Adolph! The young lady is not interested in the details of your sordid sex life.

Hitler: I voz just making ze small talk.

Jesus: I agree with you, Kerry. I myself do not indulge in any kind of sexual activity. But I must admit...I do like to tuck into a KFC bargain bucket on occasion.

Hitler: Hang on! Vot about zat party vhen you got 'out of your head' on tequila slammers unt 'had' Princess Diana in ze back bedroom?

Jesus: I didn't 'have her', you moron. I told you at the time, we were merely discussing 'conspiracy theories'.

Hitler: Ve could hear you through ze door. Don't think you can fool me. I've not heard so much screaming since Himmler took up dentistry.

Jesus: Look, shut up, will ya? You really are a.......

Hitler: Vot? Vot am I?

Jesus: *(Looking at Kerry, who is still smiling)* You're someone who needs help. That's what you are. I feel sorry for you.

Hitler: You are such a prat! 'King of kings', vot tosh!

Kerry: *(Interrupting them)* Gentleman, please. I really would like to see my husband, if it's all the same to you.

Jesus: I do apologise. Mister Hitler is a 'bit much' at times, especially when he's been 'on the sauce'. Adolph! Go and get Andy...NOW!

Hitler: *(Going to the bedroom)* I luff it vhen you are masterful.

Hitler taps on Andy's door and goes inside.

Jesus: Well, Kerry, you look like a nice girl to me. I hope you're not going to deliver another blow to our Andy. I don't think he could take another knock. I must say, you're not what I imagined from what Andy said about you but there again, Andy was describing you as a woman in her seventies and you are projecting a much younger image.

Kerry: This is what I looked like when I was in my thirties. I was a confident girl in those days. It was a good time in my life.

Jesus: Well, I hope you've got good news for our Andy. Adolph and I have been really worried about him.

Kerry: They always said, 'it's good to have a friend in Jesus'. It's nice to see that's true.

Kerry touches Jesus' hand. They smile at each other. At that moment Andy and Hitler enter the room. Kerry stands up and she and Andy look at each other for a moment. Kerry takes a step towards Andy. Andy takes a step towards Kerry. They pause for a moment and then throw their arms around each other. Hitler signals to Jesus and they both discreetly exit by the front door. Andy and Kerry break the embrace and take a good hard look at each other.

Andy: It's good to see you, Kerry.

Kerry: It's good to see you too, Andy. I have prayed for you so many times.

Andy: My God, you look gorgeous! I've seen

pictures of you looking like this but in the flesh you are simply radiant!

Kerry: Yes but remember, Andy, what you are seeing is not flesh but spirit; the light that my spirit generates here in the afterlife.

Andy: Yes, of course. It's just the way you appear. The afterlife doesn't seem to have done *you* any harm.

Kerry: It was such a relief, in the end, to slip away into the light after all the treatment and those dark days.

Andy: Well, it's nice to see one of my wives isn't a freak. I was beginning to think I was cursed. Seeing you is the first good thing that's happened to me since I got here. Well, apart from meeting my new friends. Jesus is a lovely fella and Adolph isn't as black as he's painted; he's got a heart of gold. He and Jesus wind each other up a bit but they love each other really.

Kerry: It's nice you feel that way about them. Shall we sit down?

They do.

Andy: So, what happens now? You're here and I'm here and-well, where do we *go* from here?

Pause.

Kerry: What are you looking for, Andy?

Andy: What am I looking for?

Kerry: In the afterlife?

Andy: I don't honestly know. They told me I had to make a decision about who I was going to spend eternity with and when I met Mandy and Vicky... I realised I couldn't contemplate spending an afternoon with them...let alone eternity. So, now here we are and you like a breath of fresh air, following my previous disappointments. I mean...this place...I've learnt to expect the unexpected here. For a minute there, I thought you were a giant chicken. I'm delighted to see you're not.

Kerry: A what?

Andy: It doesn't matter...

Kerry: Well, I'm not a chicken...as you can see.

Andy: Indeed not. It's just that things have been a bit strange round here. You can't help but wonder where the next big shock is going to come from.

Kerry: You can relax now: No more shocks. I'm here with you, in the light at last, to bring you everlasting peace.

Andy: That's nice.

Kerry: Just you, me and the Lord God. You can rest assured that HE will never let you down.

Andy: It's nice to see you believe so strongly in something.

Kerry: What about you, do you believe?

Andy: Believe?

Kerry: In God?

Andy: Well, if this is Heaven, then, I guess there must be a God of some kind.

Kerry: Can you feel his presence here? I could feel it the instant I arrived; something all consuming.

Andy: I can't say I've felt anything like that.

Kerry: Perhaps you need something more...direct.

Andy: 'Direct'?

Kerry: Would it help if you...saw Him?

Andy: Saw God? Gosh, is that possible?

Kerry: In a way.

Andy: How do you mean?

Kerry: You see God is pure spirit; He is a voice in all of us. When I hear Him, I like to put a face to that voice, it helps me communicate with Him. Now, as we none of us knows what God truly looks like, we have to dig deep into our imagination to find a form and that form is merely a vessel for the voice of God. Do you understand?

Andy: Err...

Kerry: It's just...well, I have found a face for Him but I don't want you to think badly of me for taking that liberty. You won't, will you?

Andy: Why should I do that? I think there's always some sort of physical representation of our perception of the way...err...religious icons and s piritual leaders are portrayed; in lots of religious art for example...

Kerry suddenly produces a glove puppet from her handbag. It is a badly knitted version of a man with a white beard. It has a moveable mouth. She holds it up. Andy looks on, his mouth agape.

Kerry: Behold. It is...The Lord!

Andy: Blood and sand!

Kerry: Is this not the most humbling experience of your whole existence?

Andy: Well, It's one of the most gobsmacking experiences of my whole existence. Mind you, 'gobsmacking experiences of my whole existence' are becoming run of the mill in this place.

Kerry: You are in His presence. He is a part of us and we are a part of Him and...

Andy: I can see where you're coming from it's just...

Kerry: What?

Andy: Well, why does He look like *that?*

Kerry: Like what?

Andy: Well, for want of a better phrase...'a wonky

looking glove puppet'.

Kerry: You are having difficulty with the physical manifestation?

Andy: Well...yes, you could put it that way.

Kerry: Is it because He's made of wool?

Andy: Yes, in part....and the fact that I suspect the person who made Him was not the most skilled in the art of 'knit one pearl one'.

Kerry: His appearance is totally irrelevant...please do not judge. This is a place where the physical image is merely illusion...nothing is real.

Andy: People keep saying that but I'm finding myself constantly confronted by a procession of increasingly bizarre characters.

Kerry: It was knitted with much love and devotion by a deeply spiritual Indian princess. It would have been uncharitable not to use it.

Andy: I suppose it could have been worse; He could have been Orville the duck, Gordon the gopher or Parker from Thunderbirds.

Kerry: Remember, the Lord follows no rule book; He moves in mysterious ways.

Andy: Especially when someone has their hand up Him.

Kerry puts the puppet to her ear.

Kerry: He wishes to speak with you now.

Andy: Speak with me?

Kerry: Are you ready?

Andy: Oh, you mean...He...The...err...glove...err... God?

Kerry: Prepare yourself.

Andy: OK. I'm ready.

Kerry: *(Adopting a booming voice)* Hello.

Andy looks on dumbfounded.

Kerry: *(As God)* Hello, Andy.

Andy :Err...'hello'. *(To Kerry)* Is it Him?

Kerry: *(As herself)* Yes.

Andy: What should I call Him?

Kerry: *(As God)* I am God: creator of all things, all knowing, all seeing, omnipresent, omnipotent, ubiquitous, ambidextrous, and wise beyond all reason. Worshiped throughout the known world under my many non de plumes.

Andy: Delighted, I'm sure.

Andy offers his hand, he stops himself.

Kerry: *(As God)* You are a deeply troubled man, Andy.

Andy: Is it any wonder?

Kerry: Has Heaven been a disappointment to you, Andy?

Andy: Is that what this is? Because if it is...it falls far short of any preconceived idea of Heaven that I ever had.

Kerry: *(as God)* What did you expect? Pearly gates, Saint Peter, people sat around on clouds playing muzak on harps?

Andy: Well, what can I say? I didn't think that everyone I would meet would be totally unhinged. I feel like the subject of some massive wind-up. I'm starting to think that God might turn out to be Jeremy Beadle.

Kerry: *(as God) laughs.*

Kerry: *(As God)* Has it been nice to be reunited with your lost loves and to rekindle old feelings?

Andy: Err...well. I don't know about 'old' feelings, I think this place has evoked feelings I never knew I had.

Kerry: *(As God)* Have you come to a decision?

Andy: About...?

Kerry: *(As God)* Your wives? Eternity?

Andy: Oh, my God!

Kerry: *(As God)* Yes.

Andy: No...I meant...

Kerry: *(As God)* Anyway...have you?

Andy: Well...Mandy is a bit too 'full on' these days and Vicky is...well...it's the little matter of the meat and two veg...

Kerry: *(As God)* That leaves wife number three...the lovely Kerry.

Andy: Yes.

Kerry: *(As God)* Is she not the image of loveliness itself?

Andy: Oh, yes.

Kerry: *(As God)* Well?

Andy: Err...

Kerry: *(As herself)* Well?

Andy: Well...

Kerry: *(As God)* WELL...?

Andy: Err, will you...that is, will He, will 'God' be... with us?

Kerry: *(Somewhat indignantly, as herself)* Why, of course: God is always with us.

Andy: I meant, will you/He be making these kind of appearances on a regular basis? I mean, what if we had people round?

Kerry: *(As herself)* Yes, you'll be delighted to hear

that we can all three be as one. God will be forever by our side.

Kerry: *(As God)* You can bet your bottom dollar on it.

Andy: Oh, my......!?

Andy gets up and talks to the audience.

Andy: Well, what do you do? I was wondering how I was going to make a choice between the three women I loved and in the end I'm left with 'Hobson's choice'. I'm seriously considering running off with the chicken. I don't know what lessons this has taught me but maybe it will teach me something about not having expectations. If the three women of my life had been the women they were......

There is a knock on the door.

Kerry: *(As herself)* Are you expecting anyone?

Andy: No. it can't be Jesus or Adolph. They'll be 'down the club'.

Andy goes to the door.

Kerry: *(As God)* At least you know it's not someone selling life insurance.

Andy opens the door, it is Eva. She is dressed in a green fairy outfit, complete with wand.

Eva: Hi.

Andy: Shiver me timbers!

Eva: It's me!

Andy: So I can see.

Eva: Can I come in?

Andy Do you have to?

Eva: Oh, don't be like that.

Eva walks in. She spins round in her fairy dress.

Eva: Well, you said you didn't believe in fairies...Ta da!

Andy: This is my wife Kerry.

Eva: Hi.

Kerry: Hello, Eva.

Kerry: *(As God)* Hello, my child.

She looks at Andy, confused. Andy shrugs, she stands there smiling.

Eva: So, are you two...err... three...getting reacquainted?

Andy: Yes.

Eva: That's nice!

She stands there grinning.

Andy: Eva, I have to tell you that since I met you, things have gone from bad to worse and the sight of you now does not exactly fill me with glee. Now, I just know you're here to deliver some cataclysmic news. So, let's just get it over with.

Eva: OK. Well, what do you want first, the good news or the bad news?

Andy: Oh, crikey. Let's have the bad news. Let's have something I'm used to. Come on; give me your best shot!

Eva: Well, the bad news is...I've just had my bottom smacked!

Andy: Is that supposed to be bad news?

Eva: Well, yeah! *(She snorts)*

Andy: That is the kind of bad news I can handle. What about the good news?

Eva: The good news is, well...it's not entirely good news, because, it's because of the good news that there's bad news, if you know what I mean. It's because of the good news, that I had my bottom smacked, which was of course the bad news, which wouldn't have even happened if there hadn't been the good news in the first place. Actually, when I said I had my bottom smacked, I didn't mean it figuratively. I meant it literally...if that's the right way round.

Andy: Will you please get to the point?

Eva: The point?

Andy: The good news!

Eva: The good news?

Andy: Yes. 'The good news' that you came specifically to tell me. *That* good news!

Eva: Oh, yeah 'the good news'! Well. Hang on; I've got it written down.

She takes a bit of paper out. She tries to read it.

Eva: Put Jimmy Savile in with Osama Bin Laden.

They all look at each other confused.

Kerry: I think that might be the wrong scrap of paper.

She pulls out another piece of paper.

Eva: Oh hang on, yeah, here it is...'You're going home'!

Andy: What?

Eva: I'm sorry! Bit of a faux pas on my part. It seems you shouldn't actually be here yet. Got a bit muddled about dates; it's always been a problem of mine. I could never understand how the twentieth century always began with a nineteen. I'm such a dizzy Lizzy.

Andy: You mean, I'm not dead?

Eva: No.

Andy: Not even slightly?

Eva: Not even an itsy witsy teeny weenie yellow polka-dot bikini bit dead.

Andy: I don't know what to say…I'm stunned!

Eva: The Grim Reaper himself summoned me in. He wasn't a happy bunny, I can tell you. He told me I have to make absolutely sure I don't make another blunder. I'm to take you back to the exact time I picked you up. I hope I don't make a 'pig's breakfast' of it. I've got it all written down in my little book of 'what's what'. Trouble is... I'm not sure where I left it.

Andy is dancing 'round the room.

Andy: I'm going home! I'm not dead! I can't believe it! I'm alive!

Eva: I just need to know *when* to take you back and…Oh yeah. I have to remember to wipe your memory of the afterlife…err… I think that's it…err… was there something else? I got distracted by a hunky fella walking past the window. That was me... gone!

Kerry rises and approaches Eva.

Kerry: Listen, Eva, I can see you're a bit stressed out by all of this. I know GR and I know what he'd do if you did make another mistake with this client.

Eva: He'd lay an egg.

Kerry: That's an understatement! Listen, let me help you out. I have a friend in a very high place, as you can see.

Eva: *(Looking at the puppet)* What...your sock drawer?

Kerry: Now, we know the client's history, and can wipe his memory and get him back where he belongs. I myself, worked as a collector when I first arrived here. With my help, we can take care of it. How does that sound?

Eva: Well, I'd like to do it meself, but, I'm as daft as a brush, that didn't get put in the cupboard with the other daft brushes on account of being too daft. So, if you can sort it... that would be brilliant! Yeah! Hang on...isn't there a rule about not collecting your own?

Kerry: That's true but I'm not collecting him, I'm *returning* him.

Eva Oh, yeah. Well, that's OK, then. Yeah. Fantastic!

Kerry Well, I'll take care of things here. You can relax now. Job done!

Eva Right.

Eva is still standing there.

Kerry: *(As God)* Thank you, Eva, you are excused.

Eva: Oh, OK. *(To Andy, with a look)* See ya.

Andy Not too soon, I hope.

Eva exits.

Kerry: Well, it seems you're not dead after all.

Andy: So it would appear. And you were a 'collector'...like Eva?

Kerry: That's right. It was my spiritual calling.

Andy: And you can get me home?

Kerry: Yes...with the help of The Almighty. Are you ready?

Andy stops.

Andy: Wait a minute. Some things still don't make sense.

Kerry: Like what?

Andy: If this is the spirit world, then how can I be here if I'm not a spirit? Aren't they all supposed to be projections of how that spirit sees itself?

Kerry: That's correct, but you *are* a spirit. You don't have to be dead to have a spirit. Eva picked up your spirit. Your body is safe and sound, waiting to be reunited with you.

Andy: Are you going to erase my memory?

Kerry: Yes. You won't remember anything about the afterlife. It will just seem like a vaguely remembered dream.

Andy: Gosh...

Kerry: Are you ready to go home?

Andy: I guess so. There is just one other thing, though. What about my friends; Adolph and Jesus. I won't get to say goodbye to them. You will tell them 'thanks for everything', and tell them to be nice to each other.

Kerry: I will, but don't expect miracles…even from Jesus.

Andy: I won't.

Kerry: I hope things work out for you, Andy. I'll see what I can do. You deserve some good fortune.

Andy: Gosh, I feel quite emotional. I feel like Dorothy in 'The Wizard of Oz'. It's like I've been here forever. It's sort of like time stands still here, isn't it?

Kerry: That's exactly what it is. We can make time stand still. You know, Andy… there's so much you could have learned about life and the afterlife. It's so complex and interesting. If you had stayed I'd have explained it to you but maybe another time. Are you ready to face your future, Andy?

Andy Well, ready as I'll ever be.

Kerry: Remember, you're going to forget all about me, Eva, Hitler, Jesus, giant chickens and everybody else you've met here.

Andy: I understand.

Kerry: *(Taking Andy's hand)* Time to go, Andy.

Kerry: *(As God)* Prepare for warp speed.

Blackout

(Alternative)

ACT TWO
Scene Four

A bedroom, full of 1960s posters. Someone is under the covers. Kerry is sitting on the bed. She has her hand resting on the covers.

Kerry: Time to wake up, Andy. You're not in Kansas anymore.

A low moan starts to come from under the covers. Andy emerges but he is a young man; in his early twenties.

Andy: Where am I? What happened? *(To Kerry, only half recognising her)* Hello.

Kerry: Hello. You're home.

Andy: Home?

Kerry: Have a look.

Andy gets out of bed, still a little bleary. He walks up to the mirror.

Andy: Oh, my God! What... Is that me?

Andy stares at himself then runs around the room picking things up.

Andy: *(at the top of his voice)* It's the sixties! Oh, my

God! I'm young! THE SIXTIES!

Kerry: Try to keep your voice down. You'll need some time to adjust to your new, or rather...old life and surroundings.

Andy: Jesus, this is incredible!

He stops himself.

Andy: Jesus?

Jesus appears in a spot, eating an Easter Egg.

Jesus: You rang. Well, I'm a bit jealous; I thought I was the only one who gets resurrected round here.

Andy: It's Jesus!

Jesus: Have a good one, Andy. Hope you enjoy your second bite of the cherry. Adolph's here; he just wanted to say goodbye.

Hitler appears in a spot, eating 'Monster Munch'.

Andy: *(To Kerry)* It's Adolph!

Hitler: Good luck, Andy. I'm just off to meet zhose buxom Hungarian fraulein's at ze Ann Summer's party. No rest for ze vicked, eh? Give her von for me...

Jesus: Oh, Adolph.

Hitler makes a crude arm gesture. Andy laughs and

smiles. Kerry waves her hand in front of Andy's face. The spots go out.

Kerry: Forget. You must forget it all.

Andy holds his head in his hands. The sound of a female voice singing 'If Paradise is Half as Nice' is heard off. For a moment Andy seems perplexed by this. He looks in the mirror again.

Andy: Is that...?

Kerry: Don't be alarmed, everything's going to be fine. Try not to over-react.

The door opens and Andy leaps in shock. The young Mandy enters. This is the Mandy, Andy had described earlier; the English rose. She is shocked at Andy's reaction.

Mandy: What on Earth's wrong? You nearly jumped out of your skin.

Andy: Mandy? It's...you!

Mandy: Of course it's me. How many more wives have you got?

Andy: *(With a look to Kerry)* You are...'The One'.

Mandy I'm glad to hear it. And you are '*a* one'...that's for sure. So, how do I look? Do you like my new outfit?

Andy: *(Still stunned)* You look gorgeous. Stunning.

Mandy: I just bought it. I'm meeting Pam.

Andy: Oh, right...Where you meeting her?

Mandy: Your memory! Are you sure you're twenty three and not seventy three? We talked about this... Wigan Pier.

Andy: Wigan Pier?

Mandy Yes. There's a lovely little French bistro just opened there.

Andy: Oh, my God!

Mandy: What's up?

Andy: *(Suddenly)* I don't want you to go...not there!

Mandy: Why not?

Andy: I...I...don't know...I have an odd feeling about it.

Mandy: Oh, Andy, I told you yesterday I was going. I've been looking forward to it.

Andy: Did you? I mean...oh yeah...you did! But that was *then*...and this is also then... except that 'then' is kind of...'now', so to speak.

Mandy: Sorry?

Andy grabs Mandy by the waist.

Andy: Don't go! I need you.

Mandy: Need me?

Andy: Yes....I need you... I'm feeling...rampant!

Mandy: That's nothing new. You're always feeling rampant.

Andy: Yes but today I'm feeling extra rampant. Like the most rampant ram in a field of extremely rampant rams.

Mandy: Andy, I promised Pam. I'll be back before you know it and you can be as rampant as you like.

Andy: But you can meet Pam anytime you like... but not today...and not there. I swear on my life I will never ask you to do this again. Pleeaaasssse.

Kerry waves a hand in front of Andy. He collapses on the bed.

Kerry: Good bye, Andy. Have a good life.

Kerry exits .Mandy goes to Andy. Andy suddenly sits up revived. He smiles at Mandy.

Mandy: Are you OK?

Andy: Never felt better.

Mandy: So, what's the problem with me going to Wigan Pier?

Andy: Oh, is that where you're going?

Mandy: Yes, to the French bistro.

Andy: Nice.

Mandy: You really are behaving very oddly. I'm going now, no more arguments, OK?

Andy: OK.

Mandy: *(Surprised at his change)* I'll see you later.

Andy: Enjoy yourself. Love you.

Mandy: Love you too.

She heads to the door, turns to look at Andy. He smiles at her. She shrugs and exits. Andy is left alone. He looks around the room. He goes to the mirror and looks at himself. He looks deep in thought.

Andy: *(Singing quietly)* If paradise is half as nice as heaven that you take me to, who needs paradise I'd rather have...you...*(Andy stops, as if a sudden thought hit him)*

Mandy enters fuming.

Mandy: Some people!

Andy: What's up?

Mandy: You wouldn't credit some people, would you?

Andy: What happened?

Mandy: As I came out, just now, some woman was slashing my tyres right in front of my face. Then she just walked calmly away.

Andy: What did you do?

Mandy: For some reason I just stood there rooted to the spot. She didn't look the type; attractive, presentable women with striking red hair.

Andy: Gosh!

Mandy: Well, after having vandalised my moped, she then had the good grace to actually apologise... and get this...she produced some god-awful glove puppet and in a deep voice she said "You'll thank me for it someday".

Andy: She sounds barking!

Mandy: You're telling me.

Andy: ...But she was right about one thing.

Mandy: Right about what?

Andy: Well, she stopped you from going out. I did say I had an odd feeling about it.

Mandy: Yes, well, I think we all know about your 'odd feelings', and they usually involve a certain part of your anatomy below the waist.

Andy: If you say so.

Mandy: I do.

Andy: Well, that's frog's legs on Wigan Pier off the menu, I suppose. I'm just trying to think what else a young married couple like us can do in a room like this, with very little furniture, no telly, a broken record player and an ample sized, reasonably robust bed.

Mandy: And what conclusion did you draw?

Andy: That's something I'd like to discuss with you if you'd like to step this way.

He takes her hand and leads her to the bed.

Mandy: Well, as I now appear to be stranded here with you, I might just have to take what you have to offer.

Andy: Sounds good to me.

Andy takes her in his arms and kisses her.

Andy: You know what, Mand?

Mandy: What?

Andy: It sure is good to be alive.

Mandy: It sure is.

They both collapse on the bed giggling.

THE END

Curtain call music: *'Spirit in the Sky' by Norman Greenbaum.*

Acknowledgements:

My gratitude to the following:

Chris Cunday.
Mavis Bailey.
Mike Russell.
The Lyceum Theatre, Oldham.
Guide Bridge Theatre.
Saddleworth Players.
The Waterloo and Crosby Theatre Company.
Violet Circle Publishing.
To cast and crew of all productions of 'Heaven Knows I'm Miserable Now'.
Those others who have helped or inspired me with my writing, you know who you are.

More Author's
From
Violet Circle Publishing

Mike Beale.
Crumble's Adventures. Children's Fiction.

Discover the wonderful world of Crumble, the little dog with a nose for friends and adventure. This delightful story is an ideal read for young children making their way into advanced reading, and also a wonderful story for mum and dad to read at bedtime.

Robin John Morgan.
Heirs to the Kingdom. Fantasy Adventure Series.

A fast paced and action packed adventure set in the future after the world is devastated by a deadly virus, bringing about the end of modern life as we know it. Join a young boy who has an unnatural talent with a long bow, as he leads a group of his woodland dwelling friends against the might of the powerful Mason Knox. This fantasy adventure takes threads of the past and weaves them into a modern, captivating, and thought provoking tale of the struggle of the woodland people, as they fight to preserve their life at peace within nature.

Ted Morgan.
Wordsmith's Wanderings. Poetry And Rhymes.

Wordsmith's Wandering is a simple delight to read. Based on the life and observations of the author this reflective and at time very humours collection of poems and rhymes, reflect the 76 years of a man who has served in national service and the health system, whilst also working as a member of the mountain rescue team.

Colin Smith.
Heaven Knows I'm Miserable Now. Stage Play

Is death really the end? Andy Reardon is about to find out, and he's beginning to wish it was. When Andy discovers his number is up, he finds the afterlife is not exactly fluffy clouds, harps, and Saint Peter.
What will Andy do about his dead wives?
He has three of them, all chomping at the bit to see Andy again but none of them are quite how Andy remembers. With Jesus Christ and Adolph Hitler dishing out advice, Andy might make the right decision, and be happy for all eternity. This black comedy takes Andy on the trip of a death time, and leaves him to make choices he'd never dream he would ever have to make.

Violet Circle Publishing, Manchester, UK.

www.ingramcontent.com/pod-product-compliance
Ingram Content Group UK Ltd.
Pitfield, Milton Keynes, MK11 3LW, UK
UKHW020226250726
13967UKWH00001B/215